PORTRAITS
OF A PRINCESS

TRAVELS WITH DIANA

All photographs appear courtesy of Kent Gavin

Design by David Bradshaw
Color reproduction by Aylesbury Studios
Printed by Butler & Tanner

www.stmartins.com

ISBN 0-312-33782-5
EAN 978-0312-33782-7

First published in Great Britain by Sidgwick & Jackson,
an imprint of Pan Macmillan Ltd

First U.S. Edition: November 2004

10 9 8 7 6 5 4 3 2 1

PORTRAITS
OF A PRINCESS
TRAVELS WITH DIANA

PATRICK JEPHSON, L.V.O.

PICTURES BY KENT GAVIN, F.R.P.S
ROYAL PHOTOGRAPHER

St. Martin's Press ≈ New York

Contents

Introduction

Diana, Princess of Wales, became 'the most famous woman in the world.' So it seems appropriate to take the world as the setting for this attempt to take a new look at her. In doing so, we have tried to capture what it was like for Diana to live through the process that turned her from Prince Charles's diffident consort into an independent, global force for good.

As the years pass since her death, it's clear that the Princess will have a prominent place in British royal history. As someone who saw this history unfold before his eyes – and even had a hand in shaping it – I make no apology for recording some of it while memories are still fresh.

For many people, Diana's memory is the lens through which the Windsors will now always be viewed. That is one reason among many why uncertainty still hangs over the long-term character and role of the monarchy. She changed our preconceived notions. In the words of the satirist Auberon Waugh – a critic who became an admirer – Diana was 'a free spirit'. As her private secretary, it was sometimes my job to try to guide Diana. I quickly saw that she defended her freedom fiercely. I also learned, sometimes painfully, that her judgement wasn't always perfect.

Nevertheless, my enduring image is of Diana using that hard-won freedom like a sword. Though her aim could be erratic, ultimately she used it to cut the ground from under her critics by the brilliance of the work she did for so many causes.

My aim in the following pages is to provide some reminders of that brilliance. For that, we have only Diana to thank. And where better to start than with an overseas trip that sums up how much we had to be thankful for, not so long ago…

Australia and New Zealand, 1982

This Australia and New Zealand tour has acquired a special place in royal folklore. It was the ideal depiction of the bright new dawn of monarchy. The handsome Prince, his perfect bride and their adorable baby son all playing happily on a rug in the Antipodean sunshine. Little did we know that it marked not a beginning but an end. The end of an age of happy innocence for the Royal Family whose secrets had, until then, been safely hidden behind palace walls, and for their loyal subjects who didn't want things to change.

There was little talk then of an Australian republic, and no talk at all of the fairytale marriage turning sour. We had absolutely no inkling of the jealousy, rivalry, separation and divorce to come. Not in our worst night-mares did we picture the gun carriage and its flag-draped burden arriving for the funeral at Westminster Abbey.

So enjoy these pictures as souvenirs of that bygone age. As we look at the images that follow, it's worth noting that events needn't have turned out as they did. If the bride and groom had been able to give each other more and take less, if the Royal Family had found a way to adapt to the newcomer, if the divorcees had been able to turn their bitterness to reconciliation, if… if…

But it did turn out badly. As badly as it could. And, it seems, the British Royal Family is condemned to live in Diana's shadow indefinitely and destined to endure repeatedly the crises that look like being her legacy to them. Trials, tapes and tittle-tattle have been her bequest not just to Charles and Camilla, but to the tarnished ideal of the monarchy.

Luckily that's not the end of the story. The Princess I knew was not the self-obsessed, self-pitying victim of Andrew Morton's *Diana: Her True Story*. Nor was she the dark-eyed avenger of the notorious *Panorama* interview. Those were undeniable aspects of her character – to omit mention of these or other, more mundane human failings would be to dismiss her as a

Above: The Royal Family's future looked bright when this photo was taken during the hugely popular Australia and New Zealand tour of 1983. Opposite: In period costume, Canada, 1985.

saccharin invention – but they were not the whole person. The Diana I knew overcame these traits every day she stepped out of her palace and used her talents to brighten the lives of others. In the process, she brightened her own life too.

That strong, perceptive and sympathetic woman is the hero of this book. It's time she ceased being a shadow over the Windsors' future and instead became a light – a light that might even reveal ways to make the Royal Family's unenviable burden of duty just a little bit easier to bear. And if for nobody else, let that light illuminate the way ahead for the infant who was the centre of that happy family portrait in the New Zealand sun. If these pictures, and maybe even some of these words, make that more likely, that will be a bonus.

Above Braemar Games. Diana had great respect and affection for the Queen but sadly light-hearted moments like this one were not often repeated. Right: Dancing in Australia, 1983.

FOREWORD
THE VIEW FROM INSIDE THE PRESS PEN
BY KENT GAVIN

1980 was a turning point in my career. I was chief photographer of the *Daily Mirror* when editor Mike Molloy and picture editor Len Greener asked me to spend a little time checking out a young girl by the name of Lady Diana Spencer. It was rumoured that she was romantically linked with the Prince of Wales. An unusual assignment, to say the least.

I had by now won the British Press Photographer of the Year award three times, and was travelling the world covering major news and features. Little did I know that I was to spend the next 18 years of my life photographing Diana. My pictures of her would win me Royal Photographer of the Decade for the 1980s and then for the 1990s, and Royal Photographer of the Year seven times until her death in Paris on 31 August 1997. Until 1 September 1997, I enjoyed every moment.

In those early days, a handful of staff photographers were employed full time on royal work. Each newspaper would assign a photographer and reporter with the sole duty of covering her engagements as Lady Diana, and later as Princess of Wales, in the UK, overseas and even on holiday. These overseas assignments were eventually known as Windsor Tours.

By the time she became engaged to Prince Charles, everything Diana did was being photographed, no matter how mundane or unimportant it seemed. Even if everyone thought it'd be a dull engagement, we would turn up to see what she was wearing. Fleet Street editors had become besotted with her as they saw their circulation figures rising. Putting a picture of Diana on the front page sold more copies, and that in turn made her a fashion icon.

I had an instant liking for her. Taking her picture was a delight. Diana soon became very aware of the photographers who became her constant travelling companions, and was on first name terms with them. By the same token, she soon realised the difference between official photographers and the paparazzi, or 'paps', who gave her so much grief as they tried to make money out of her and her private life.

I had a very good working relationship with Diana. Once I was sitting

Previous page: Hilton Hotel, 1993. Diana's emotional 'Time and Space' speech made headlines but didn't solve long-term questions over her role. Opposite: First day of the honeymoon. HMY *Britannia*, Gibraltar. Next page: Diana is now a future queen, a royal superstar, a mother… and still 21.

Top left: What might have been... a reassuring picture of family togetherness. Top right and bottom left: I was chosen to take the official christening portraits of Prince William. Buckingham Palace, 4 August 1982.

behind her in London's Haymarket Theatre watching *The Phantom of the Opera*. During the interval she told me that Prince Charles was snowed in at Sandringham, and that he would not be able to attend Prince William's first day at school. I nipped out at the start of the second half to file the story. And it's because I got on with her so well that she chose me to photograph Prince William's christening at Buckingham Palace.

I also recall several personal moments with her on tour, like when we were travelling back from New York on Concorde and she asked her lady-in-waiting to invite me forward to sit next to her. We had a very informal chat for over an hour, and again on the trip back from Pakistan when we discussed the trip.

Soon the foreign tours were taking me abroad for up to five months a year. The tours to Australia and New Zealand were long but exciting. Some of the locations tested me professionally, for example Ayers Rock in Australia, the Taj Mahal in India and the Pyramids in Egypt. I remember joking with her when we asked her to pose with the Giza Pyramids that one of the seven wonders of the world now had the eighth beside them, and she looked at me with those beautiful blue eyes and a smile that said it all.

For the early foreign trips I took several long lenses – 800mm, 500mm and 300mm, and other short and zoom lenses, satellite phones and darkroom equipment. The excess baggage charges were horrendous. However, as technology changed, everything – especially the transmission of pictures – became easier. I often think how easy it would have been with today's digital technology. My equipment now is two Canon DS 1 digital cameras, three zoom lenses, standard 29–85mm lens, 85–200mm and 35–350mm with two flash guns with high-speed battery, a laptop and mobile phone with ISDN transmission. It's a far cry from those early days.

In the 1980s and '90s, the Princess was attracting up to as many as thirty or forty photographers per assignment in the UK. What with that and the ever-increasing crowds, I needed another piece of equipment, a small, metal stepladder. I had to arrive early to place it in the front row to get

Opposite bottom right: The kiss that missed, Jaipur, India, Valentine's Day, 1992. Accident or design? It didn't matter – away from the cameras, Charles and Diana are already living separate lives.

15

the best position if I was not on the royal rota. (Under the rota system, a restricted number of photographers was given access by the Palace when space was limited. Rota passes were shared among us in turn. We then had to make our pictures available to the rest of the media.)

Media arrangements for the official visits abroad, as with those in the UK, were co-ordinated by the Princess's press secretaries. I worked with them all, including Victor Chapman, Dicky Arbiter and Geoff Crawford. Victor had the knack of being able to work with both the press and the Palace, and wasn't afraid to express his views to the media and his royal employers. Charles liked him immensely. Victor later died from cancer.

It was not an easy task for press secretaries to handle the increasing demands of photographers. All in all, we staff photographers had a good relationship with them, though they certainly had their work cut out with the 'paps'. And then you had reputable freelance photographers such as Tim Graham and Robin Nunn. They also had a very good working relationship with press secretaries and the Princess. She knew which ones she could trust.

She once told me how a 'pap' chased her into a London taxi shouting and swearing at her, saying he had to pay for his mortgage and children's school fees. The photograph showed her kneeling on the floor of the cab, crying.

I quickly came to despise the street paparazzi. In my view they were not photographers at all. I explained this to Diana and fortunately she knew the difference between their methods and those of the regular Fleet Street professionals, several of whom she had grown to trust. Some of their work – mine included, I hope – she even came to admire.

My editor, Richard Stott, was a great Diana supporter, and he always asked at the morning editorial conference what Diana was doing that day. In later years Piers Morgan, his successor, encouraged me to cover all her public engagements. In fact, Piers later met Diana and Prince William at Kensington Palace to discuss ways of minimising media pressure on her

Opposite: Diana at the Pyramids, 1992. A royal emissary in her own right.

boys. Eventually this led to all the British newspaper editors giving an undertaking not to intrude on William and Harry during their school years.

The different newspaper staff and senior photographers got on very well, despite the fact that we were in competition. We soon worked out that when spending so much time together, trying to cover the same story, it was easier to pool our resources than to compete, especially on her holidays when we needed to hire boats and planes and keep down costs. There were even occasions when we filed stories for each other so that no-one missed out.

Once, when we were in Canada, Diana fainted at an exhibition on the last engagement of the tour. This was an important news photograph, and I missed it because I had already left to await her arrival in Tokyo the next day. When I got to Tokyo there were messages from my editor. Incredibly, he had even got a request to the pilot of my plane, asking him to turn it back to Canada (as if!). I did try to explain why I had gone ahead to Tokyo, in case there had been an equally newsworthy shot. When Victor Chapman told Diana what had happened, and that we had all gone to Tokyo and missed the fainting story, she thought it very funny. In the end, so did I. Even if I had stayed behind in Canada, I'd have been in the wrong location and would have missed the picture.

Another time, we staff photographers and reporters of Fleet Street's finest decided to hire a boat to sleep twelve to try and follow Charles and Diana on the yacht *Alexander*, during a Greek island cruise. We failed miserably. In two weeks spent cruising the Aegean and Mediterranean, we never had one sighting. We later found out that the skipper of our boat was a friend of the captain of the *Alexander*, so we never had a prayer. But it was a memorable assignment for other reasons, even if it didn't go down too well with our editors.

Diana's holidays were always a little tricky because they were her private time but, thanks to the help of her protection officers, we came to an arrangement – she'd give us five to ten minutes each morning and we, the

Opposite: Diana and the Duchess of Kent attend an event to mark the 40th anniversary of the Queen's accession to the throne, Earls Court, November 1992.

staff photographers, would leave her alone to enjoy the rest of the day. This worked perfectly and I, being the one that Diana seemed to trust the most, had the job of explaining to the foreign press that this was a good arrangement and in all our interests. They went along with it.

One of my pictures in particular stands out. It was the day that Diana announced she was giving up public duties in a speech at the Hilton Hotel, in London (the famous 'time and space' speech on 3 December, 1993). As she left the building, I crossed to the opposite side of the press pen and took her picture against a backdrop of photographers. Her head was down and she looked sad. But I sensed she knew there would still be a role for her.

Diana's last holiday in St Tropez was never to be forgotten. Yet again Fleet Street hired a boat, and moored it off Al Fayed's yacht and villa which Diana was using with Dodi. Diana's reaction was a mixture of fun and games. One minute she was walking down to the sea front, giving us picture opportunities, and the next she would hide.

Next day she approached our boat to speak to us, asking why we were there. We explained that the holiday had become a news story because of Mohamed Al Fayed's involvement. I felt very sorry for her. I could see she had tears in her eyes as she said, 'You will be surprised what I will do next!' This baffled us. An hour later Diana appeared on a jet-ski with Harry. They buzzed around our boat, letting us take as many pictures as we wanted.

Little was I to know that two weeks later, at 2am on 1 September, 1997, I would get a call from the office to say that Diana and Dodi had been involved in a car crash. I was in the office by 2.45am to see the pictures appearing from Paris of the accident. Soon I knew they were both dead. At first the French paparazzi were blamed for giving chase, though the inquiry found the accident was caused by drunken driving. The photographers were cleared.

I was asked to go to Paris immediately, but I explained I should stay in

Top right: What might have been... the perfect future King and Queen. Opposite bottom: Diana's empathy with sick children was legendary. Less visible – but in her eyes, just as important – was the comfort she tried to give their families.

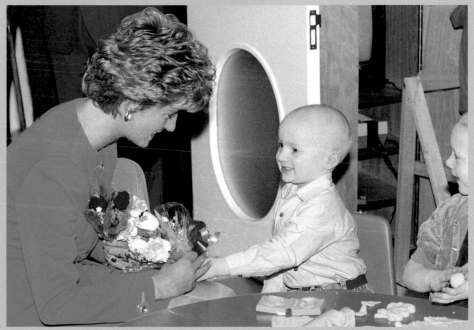

London to assist editor Piers Morgan with background information and pictures. I also guessed Diana would be flown home to London that day. So I was at Northolt airbase to see the Prince of Wales bring Diana's coffin home. It was a sight I will never forget. As the Royal Air Force pall-bearers carried her off the plane, I had a tear in my eye and a lump in my throat as I photographed the scene thinking of the last eighteen years.

Diana had the common touch and a natural ability to treat life's saddest victims as human beings first; she was a great ambassador for the nation; a woman of courage and kindness; a deeply loving mother; a princess for all time. To me she was without doubt the People's Princess who gave so much happiness to the world, especially children and people in need. A woman who brought hope and happiness to every hospice, children's home and AIDS centre she visited. I was just so pleased to have been there to record it all with my cameras.

With special thanks to Daily Mirror editors Mike Molloy, Richard Stott, Roy Greenslade and Piers Morgan.

Picture editors Len Greener, Ron Morgans and Ian Down.

Researchers Duncan Lovett, Dave Adams, John Churchill, John Mead, Gary Larkin, Peter Cook and all those at the Daily Mirror who are too many to mention by name.

And of course James Whitaker, Daily Mirror Royal Correspondent, my travelling companion for eighteen years.

Opposite: A master class in modesty. Climbing out of a vaporetto, Venice 1995.

Above: Diana excelled at mainstream, traditional royal work, here visiting a British bomber crew in Germany. Bottom: The Prince's polo accident sparked stories that the couple were close again. Despite hopeful pictures like this, the truth was very different. Cirencester Hospital, June 1990.

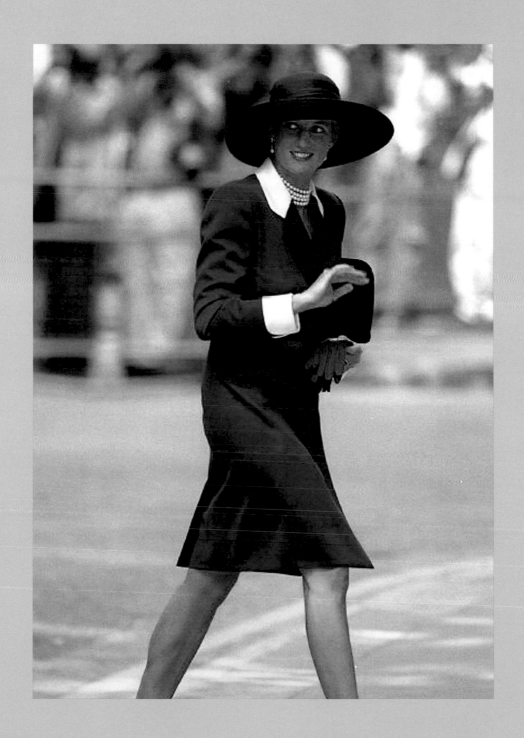

PART 1 PRINCESS OF HEARTS

'She helped me to help the poor
and that's the most beautiful thing.'

Mother Teresa

Diana perfected her crowd-pleasing style on mainstream royal engagements in the UK.

All Diana's greatest strengths, all the elements that combined to create her royal star quality, were on clearest view when she was allowed to display them on her overseas tours. It wasn't just the exotic destinations, the photogenic hosts or the eye-catching fashions. It wasn't even the media spotlight that shone relentlessly on her, every step of the way. It was that the challenges – physical as much as mental – of performing for a foreign audience gave her talents an extra edge. To see the Princess of Wales in an African refugee camp, at a Manhattan fashion award or taking tea with the President of France was to see her at the top of her game.

What wasn't so visible, but which from my position in the wings was pretty obvious, was that such world beating class had its roots back in the much less exotic turf of her own backyard. The grey, rainy skies of urban Britain rather than the blazing sun of Egypt or the grandeur of the Himalayas helped forge Diana, the international superstar. The compassion that comforted an Asian leper had been discovered in a Lancashire hospice. The courage that let her walk in a Balkan minefield had been tested in the streets of Belfast. The royal style that rocked Buenos Aires had already won hearts and applause in Leeds and Bradford.

For many people, and certainly me, this was a vital part of Diana's appeal. Though the world might elevate her to the level of deified icon, the reality was that she learned her trade back home in the inner cities and rural market towns of the UK.

Sure, they weren't the slums of Calcutta where Mother Teresa grew to sainthood. But they weren't the safely predictable world of drawing rooms, fund-raising events and polo matches that Diana had been expected to inhabit as a demure appendage to the heir to the throne. Which may explain why the Princess and Mother Teresa didn't make such an incongruous partnership when you saw them talking (and, yes, praying) together as I did. I didn't see much rapport between them at a personal level. The differences in culture and personality – not to mention height – were too great. Yet in their very separate ways it was possible to

'She was an inspiring leader – perceptive, considerate, hardworking and well organised.'

recognise the power they had in common: the power to inspire huge amounts of good.

It was that power that ultimately made working for Diana so worthwhile. She never claimed to be a saint, and she knew full well that at times she could be very difficult to serve – capricious, manipulative, demanding and frustrating. Luckily, more often she was an inspiring leader – perceptive, considerate, hard working and well organised. She was also funny, occasionally at inappropriate moments but also, defiantly, whenever the chips were down. It was these sunnier, sometimes heroic aspects of her personality that made her worth sticking with through thick and thin. They also made it possible to see her as an unlikely, but beautiful and effective force for good. No wonder she polled only just behind Winston Churchill in the BBC's Greatest Britons survey. And it all started, for me, in the Essex seaside town of Frinton.

There couldn't be a greater contrast with the slums of Calcutta, the beaches of the Caribbean, the wilderness of Africa or the Oval Office of the White House. Nevertheless, unfashionable Frinton, synonymous with genteel retirement and a steadfast rejection of anything trendy or progressive, symbolised a fixed point in Diana's frenetic progress. Frinton – and a thousand places like it – is where the British Royal Family does its first and foremost duty, reassuring ordinary Britons that their archaic constitutional monarchy is better than any alternative.

In early 1988, when I joined Charles and Diana's staff as an equerry on loan from the Royal Navy, there was no question that she would do her duty as an integral member of the royal team. An equerry is a pretty

Opposite: William's debut. Cardiff, St David's Day, 1992.

30

humble form of life in the royal household, but I didn't care. The job entailed running the day-to-day aspects of the Princess's public duties and, after several years at sea, it made a fascinating change of scene. I was expecting to go back to the navy – a career I loved – but fate, and Diana, intervened.

In late 1989, just as my two-year attachment was due to finish, it became clear to Diana that the existing office organisation – under which she and Charles shared a private secretary – was going to need restructuring. Inevitably, under the old system, things were arranged primarily to suit Charles's priorities, interests and convenience. She and her handful of staff were seen as a bit of an afterthought and, inevitably, of secondary importance.

These uncomfortable realities hadn't yet struck me as I joined the Princess for the short helicopter flight to the Essex seaside, to spend three and a half hours meeting the residents of Frinton. This was my first out-of-town engagement with the Princess – what we called an 'away day'. In the normal run of royal business it would pass almost unnoticed.

The glamorous young Princess – our future queen, don't forget – was warmly welcomed. The county's Lord Lieutenant, looking rather embarrassed in his uniform and sword, presented the traditional line-up of civic dignitaries and their spouses. A little girl presented flowers. Schoolchildren waved flags. The press cameras captured another tabloid-pleasing Di day. The sun shone. It seemed perfect. And so it was, especially if, like me, you didn't want to believe the whispers about the fairytale royal marriage being in trouble. Remember, this was when formal separation, let alone divorce, was an unimaginable option for the future king.

At that time we still all hoped and believed that Charles and Diana, if not perhaps in the first flush of love, would at least settle down to some version of long-term domestic harmony. History was full of examples of royal couples finding compromises that enabled them to keep up appearances for

Scenes from a royal apprenticeship.

Top: An eloquent portrait of a marriage in trouble. Bottom left: Diana always said she got most value from talking with older people. She was a diligent patron of Help The Aged and HelpAge International. Bottom right: An illusion of togetherness, Cardiff, 1992.

the sake of the children, and uphold the reputation of the ruling family in the eyes of its subjects.

My job, as the new cog in the machine, was to help them through their daily routine. But as time passed, the happy naivety of my first few months at St James's Palace was stripped away bit by bit. The marriage wasn't just in trouble, it was dead. And so was any real likelihood that the Prince and Princess could sustain the kind of marital charade that had come to the rescue of their forbears.

As we now know, Diana wasn't going to play second fiddle to a royal mistress even if that option might have spared her, and the rest of us, a decade of trauma that ended in her death. With more than a little help from fate, from about the time of Frinton onwards she found herself on a lonely new path that took her further and further away from the royal mainstream and into uncharted territory. And that territory, it turned out, included much of the rest of the world. As she famously said, it was the only place that she wanted to be any kind of queen.

Within three years of that Frinton visit she was irrevocably set on her new course, separating from Charles, outsmarting her enemies and outperforming her royal in-laws at their own game. The woman known formally as Her Royal Highness The Princess of Wales was rapidly becoming a major public figure in her own right and, with the exception of the Queen, didn't see herself as secondary to anyone, least of all her husband. It could not be long, she knew, before the influence of Camilla Parker-Bowles and other third parties finally destroyed what remained of her marriage. But first she needed to establish her own organisation, responsive to her needs and answerable to her as its head.

That's where I came in. I had been at least an adequate equerry; I had been tested and knew the ropes. I was ambitious, but Diana knew that I viewed the royal establishment with respect but no particular awe. Best of all, I laughed at her jokes and told her a few new ones. Ultimately she knew she needed someone, and I was the devil she knew.

Opposite: Fun with fashion, Japan, 1991. Above: An untypical but obviously amusing slip as Diana and the Queen's outfits inadvertently match. Canadian War memorial, Green Park, London 1995.

Top left: Personal photography was frowned upon. Top right: Diana broke new ground with her commitment to AIDS causes. Others in the royal establishment were puzzled by her concern for what was then a controversial and deeply unfashionable condition. But Diana knew she could use her popularity to change public attitudes. Opposite: Walkabouts were always good for morale – for visitor and visited alike. But they could be exhausting so it was good planning to keep them short and sweet, as happened here in Blackpool, 1991.

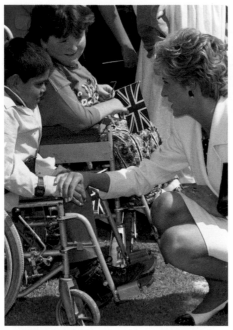

Compassion and humour always shone through in Diana's public work. In particular she never forgot the importance of getting down to eye level.

So she asked me to leave the navy and set up her own independent office as her first and, as it turned out, only private secretary. This made me the head of her independent household and ostensibly her guide. I say ostensibly because we didn't have any maps to show us the way, just a rather wobbly moral compass that hopefully would indicate where the new, independent Princess could do most good.

I was excited and terrified. Excited because, professionally, this job was the top of the tree and gave me the authority and scope to develop Diana's role in any one of a hundred worthwhile directions. But at the same time it terrified me, not just because if I screwed up everybody would notice, but because I already know that Diana and mainstream royalty were on diverging tracks. With my foot in both camps, sooner or later I would be performing a painful version of the splits. Which is what happened, eventually, and I resigned. But in the six years before that happened I was determined to reinforce the image of Diana the-queen-in-waiting as often as I could. And it reinforced my position too.

When historians judge the last decade of Diana's life, they will find the same qualities I saw in her at Frinton: her instinctive royal touch, compassion, beauty and courage. And, since the historians will not have witnessed it for themselves, let me add her ability to cheer everybody up with a joke. What kind of joke? Think of one that makes you blush – it was probably in her collection.

* * * * *

Diana was truest to her calling when working her home patch. That's why it's worth a small digression to picture her in any one of a score of British locations. Like Stirling, for example, in 1990.

The ancient capital of Scotland – midway between Glasgow and Edinburgh – was a bit ambivalent towards the Royal Family. Nationalism was on the rise. Royalty's famous affection for the Highlands won few

Another day, another routine engagement. Diana's popularity was built on the bedrock of unglamorous hard work.

hearts in the central belt. But like many places around the world, it seemed that Stirling was prepared to make an exception of Diana. The anti's allowed themselves a peek at a media phenomenon without having to swap sides. A royal rebel could still strike a sympathetic chord in the town through which Bonnie Prince Charlie had swept on his bid to throw the Hanoverians off the British throne.

At the university the few protestors failed to meet Diana's frank, blue-eyed gaze. In the town centre the main street had to be closed to traffic as thousands tried to shake her hand, give her flowers or small gifts for her sons, or just stood and stared. As Diana's increasingly individual royal style attracted more and more admirers, a new, mostly young and female constituency began to see in her someone who seemed to understand, and even share, the trials of their daily lives.

It's just another walkabout, I told myself, as I followed a couple of paces behind her. The Princess's eye-view of a walkabout crowd is an arresting sight with so many faces demanding attention, so many outstretched hands, so much visible affection, so much noise.

'Your Highness! Diane! Di! Over here, Diane!'

Di-Anne? It was true. All over the country, crowds would call out to her Di-Anne. At first I thought it disrespectful or ignorant. Or perhaps they liked the idea of a hybrid Princess of Wales-cum-Princess Royal. It would have been a winner. Later I realised it was a type of intimacy. They were making her their own.

It was clear, if she could have this effect on dour, Jacobite Stirling there was probably no limit to the number of royal sceptics she could reach out to. The embarrassment on the faces of the protestors had been eloquent enough. How could you compete with such a tall, blonde vision who sized you up with such friendly, appraising eyes?

I knew how difficult it could be to confront her. She had a special technique for dealing with potential opposition. Remember, her normal view of the world was of people rushing towards her, eyes alight with adoration, arms stretched out to take whatever she could give them. But somewhere at the back of the crowd, or lurking in a corner of a packed reception room, there would be a few determinedly unimpressed faces. They belonged to the unconverted and unconvinced – people who couldn't bring themselves to miss the excitement, but who couldn't bring themselves to be swept along by it either.

Diana could spot them at fifty yards and, ignoring for a moment the eager faces that pressed around her, would fix the doubters with that penetrating gaze. It was a challenge few could resist, especially the men. Before she left, they would find their way 'accidentally' to the front of the crowd or cluster near her car. Their reward was a special handshake, an extra word and a winning smile. She won every time.

Not long after Stirling, the Princess was due to make a St David's Day visit to Cardiff. Somehow, the Welsh Patron Saint's day had slipped through the Prince of Wales' schedule. It was the sort of opportunity Diana was beginning to exploit. Her motive was to frustrate what she saw as a growing wish on the part of Charles's supporters to diminish her role. It was another challenge she couldn't pass up.

As reinforcement for what was becoming a high-profile 'away day' she decided to take William, now aged 10, on what would be his first major royal engagement. It was a powerful expression of her determination to play her part in teaching the young Prince her version of the art of kingship. This was the signal for Charles to take an eleventh-hour interest in his wife's plans and, in double-quick time, what had been a potential Diana coup had become a painfully contrived family outing. As was now often the case, the royal couple would arrive in a nominal show of togetherness and leave separately.

The welcoming citizens of Cardiff were happily unaware of tensions behind the scenes. If they were worried by tabloid stories of royal rifts, the image of father, mother and son apparently united at the special service in Llandaff Cathedral must have been wonderfully reassuring. Unfortunately, it

Top: 'Diane! Diane!' called the crowds in Stirling The ancient capital of Scotland gave the Princess an unforgettable welcome. Bottom: In June 1992, Belfast's Falls Road was practically a war zone, especially for a member of the British Royal Family. Diana's spontaneous walkabout took real courage – and was appreciated all the more.

was exactly the sort of image that Diana saw as misleading and, ultimately, dishonest.

After the cathedral service, a helicopter took Charles away so that he could resume his re-jigged agenda that had been altered to allow for his stop-off in Cardiff. Diana and William, meanwhile, travelled into the city centre which was packed with fans. There, amidst the kind of welcome that Wales keeps for the royal people who carry its name, the young Prince signed the City Hall visitors book.

Outside, the murmur of the crowds had risen to a crescendo. Inside, William prepared to face his first walkabout. I watched as his mother stooped to give him a word of reassurance and advice. If walkabouts were an Olympic sport, Diana would have been the world's gold medal winner and top coach. Suddenly we were outside in the glare of the midday sun. The streets around the City Hall had been closed to traffic with crowd barriers set up along the route. Every inch of barrier was now lined 10-deep. The decibels wouldn't have been out of place at the old Cardiff Arms Park on match day.

After the cool tranquillity of the City Hall, the light, noise and sea of faces broke over you in a wave of sensations. With a shock, I tried to imagine what the experience must feel like to the boy who, beside the tall figure of his mother, was calmly taking in the extraordinary scene. Every voice in the crowd seemed to be calling his name. Disabled people had places of honour in the front row, recalling an almost medieval belief in miraculous royal healing powers. Through a blaze of dentures a gaggle of elderly ladies was entreating him to come to them first. Tom Jones might have run in the opposite direction. Not William. Following his mother's gentle advice, he squared his shoulders in the trademark blue blazer, and set himself determinedly to do what may be his lifetime's work. He was well up to the task. Generations of breeding combined with the shining example of his mother who, greeting the crowd with her own relaxed style, seldom took her eyes off his progress. He did her proud.

'You know, it's strange. Every other mother in the country is warning her children not to talk to strangers. And here's me telling mine that's exactly what they have to do.'

Later, on the plane back to London, I said as much. William was more concerned with his lunch which he not so surreptitiously supplemented from my plate. His mother reprimanded him for such daylight robbery, but he was unabashed. And why not? Extra lunch was small compensation for being made to go through that.

After he had gone to look at the cockpit, the Princess was good humoured enough to agree. Then, as we discussed how well the second-in-line to the throne had done at his debut, she added a sobering thought. 'You know, it's strange. Every other mother in the country is warning her children not to talk to strangers. And here's me telling mine that's exactly what they have to do.'

In fact, being a member of the Royal Family requires more courage than it has for a generation or more. There is always some degree of risk of a politically motivated attack or the actions of an isolated psychotic. Protection officers find the over-enthusiastic fan can be a worry, too. And in addition, several times a week the modern members of the Royal Family have to summon up the guts to appear in public to present a version of themselves that fits the popular requirement. It's what our constitution expects of them and, quite rightly, they regard it as an unenviable duty.

They also need the courage to withstand the attentions of a voracious media, always eager to extract maximum commercial advantage from any royal story that will boost circulation. In part, they brought this on

47

themselves with the unwise decision to bid for TV popularity in the late 1960s. And, of course, members of the Royal Family – notably Charles and Diana – either in person or through surrogates, resorted to briefing newspapers to gain advantage against each other. Since Diana's death, the Prince has refined the briefing process by using political-style spin doctors to manipulate royal headlines on royal stories concerning, for example, Prince William.

Diana embodied all the usual forms of royal courage, though at times I knew she was perilously close to losing her nerve. As well as braving the crowds, she was also conducting a covert but high-risk media campaign for popular support. Co-operating with Andrew Morton to publicise her side of the 'War of the Waleses' was, in retrospect, either a PR master-stroke or an act of gross betrayal, according to your viewpoint. My courtier's neutrality was biased in her favour. Either way, such a strategy required steady nerves.

I knew Diana had steady nerves. I had been with her in 1992 when she became the first major royal figure in decades to make an impromptu walk-about in Belfast. And not just in a secure shopping precinct but on a public road, at a time when Ulster was still effectively a war zone. And I had been with her when she stood, for an interminable two-minute silence, at the head of the officials paying their respects at the Remembrance Sunday service at Enniskillen. The scars of the recent bomb, which had killed a dozen people at that spot, were still all too visible on the buildings.

I had also followed her through the gates of mental hospitals, home to the criminally insane, so that, as patron of the country's biggest mental health charity, she could learn about such establishments for herself. But I did not follow her – and nor, at her request, did any of the nursing staff – when she joined a closed session of the patients' committee at Broadmoor. But I heard, as the heavy door closed behind her, the laughter that greeted her remarks to break the tension.

I had seen her screw up her courage and overcome a natural

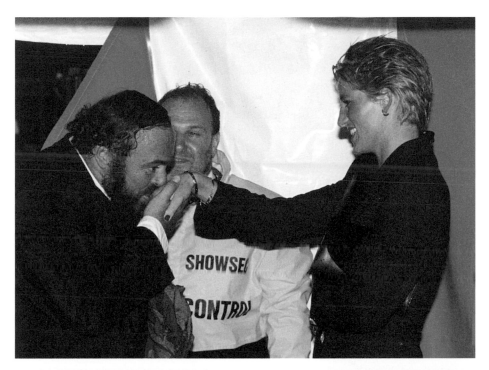

Previous spread: Hungary, 1990. Some journalists called this tour a second honeymoon. Nice idea but… Above: Party in the Park, Hyde Park, London, 1991. Charles and Diana could still be an unbeatable double act.

diffidence at the mike to become a competent public speaker. Then she found even more courage to talk about deeply personal subjects such as her battle with eating disorders. And I was there at Barrow-in-Furness when she faced down a mob of shouting anti-nuclear protestors as, despite her own misgivings, she did her royal duty by naming a missile submarine.

Most unforgettably, I was there when a man lunged at her out of the crowd in Newcastle, managing to get a hand on her before being dragged away. Pausing for only a moment to compose herself, she pressed on with the work. Just as she pressed on with a speaking engagement, despite her car being mobbed by angry demonstrators in London who mistook her dark blue Jaguar for the Prime Minister's. The image of the protection officer's hand poised, ready on his concealed pistol, will always remind me of the risks the Princess ran.

But then I suppose such displays of fortitude shouldn't come as a surprise. Becoming the most celebrated bride of the 20th century was not for the faint-hearted. Fifteen years later, becoming the most celebrated divorcee wasn't much easier.

* * * * *

Diana took her duties as Colonel in Chief very seriously. Top: Visiting the Royal Hussars in Germany Bottom: With the Royal Hampshire regiment on anti-terrorist duty in Northern Ireland.

So what of her compassion? The woman who wanted to be 'Queen in people's hearts' has become forever associated with good causes. But to what extent was she genuinely concerned about the wellbeing of others, and how much was this concern a publicity stunt?

It would be nice to say that all the compassion I saw was genuine, but sadly I can't. To pretend that her compassion was limitless would be to suggest she was a human saint. That was something she would have certainly denied – as soon as she had stopped laughing. What's more, there's no need to pretend. The real Diana was quite remarkable enough without having to invent virtues that she didn't possess. Nor is it necessary to exaggerate her qualities.

Yes, Diana could be manipulative. Some of her well-publicised interventions in personal tragedies sprang from reading about them in the *Daily Mail*. So-called 'private', caring visits to the modest homes of the affected families soon became powerful tabloid support for the pro-Diana lobby. And I more than once accompanied her on visits to the homeless in 'cardboard city' in Waterloo Bullring, central London, and other blighted areas of the capital such as the back streets of King's Cross. The visits were undeniably educational for Diana (and me), and they seemed at least to provide brief entertainment for those she met. But I knew – and, I suspect, we all knew – that the media coverage that would inevitably follow stacked up plenty of points in her favour.

Other benign examples of such double-edged compassion were timed to coincide with what Diana saw as her incarceration at Balmoral for the annual Royal Family holiday. She ordered – and I arranged – short-notice visits to hospices in Blackpool and Hull. They undoubtedly encouraged the staff and comforted patients. But we all knew an equally desired outcome was the discomfort of the rest of the family, enjoying their Highland break.

It's important to point out that, though the underlying motive had more to do with manipulating the media than compassion, such visits also did

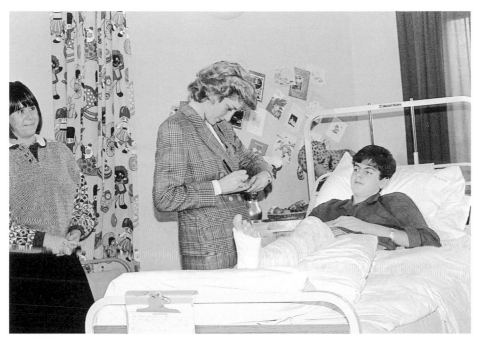

achieve a lot of good. Such manipulation was relatively easy to excuse, given the increasingly hostile noises coming from the royal establishment and its defenders in the media. Diana may have felt forced to play a little dirty but, to me, she was more sinned against than sinning. She may have famously recruited the *Daily Mail* correspondent Richard Kay to champion her cause in Fleet Street but she never called upon her paid officials to make such moral compromises on her behalf.

So, if Diana's tendency to be manipulative was certainly unattractive and risked backfiring – which it sometimes did – it was perhaps a necessary response to the unhappy situation in which she found herself. *Diana: Her True Story* wasn't anything like the whole truth. But, as a picture of how Diana saw her own predicament, especially when in self-pitying mood, it echoes my own impressions at the time. Perhaps that's why, despite all the evidence of her very human faults, people were always happy to give Diana the most precious gift a public figure can desire: forgiveness.

What about the other major criticism regularly aimed at Diana – that she was a self-obsessed fraud? It's perhaps worth recognising that, by definition, to be royal is also to be to some extent self-obsessed. That isn't to say that all our Royal Family are egomaniacs. But, even if being called Highness and having people curtsey and defer to you as your birthright doesn't make you just a little self-important, then a glance at the job description might.

In the modern British constitution the Royal Family – excluding the monarch – has no definable role at all. Its members, therefore, largely decide what the role requires of them and get on with it as they see best, with mixed results. But, ultimately, their only function is to exist and reproduce. This is hardly Louis XIV's 'L'état c'est moi' royal mission statement. But it's recognisably related. Since fulfilling these requirements involves splendid lifestyles which attract obsessive interest, it's easy to see why modern royalty is often as resented as it is envied, pitied or respected.

Diana never saw her royal status as a birthright. She knew she had to earn it through her actions. It was either an opportunity to do good and, therefore, be grasped, or a burden to be suffered. And – being the free spirit she was – that suffering would not always be borne in silence.

There, in a nutshell, is the Princess I knew for eight years. Part of her was a shining force for good, daily renewing her claim on people's affections with new ways to exploit her royal status for the benefit of others. And part of her was always a suffering child, weighed down by expectations she hadn't asked for, and angered by injustices she hadn't deserved.

A fraud? The answer lies in these pictures.

Opposite and above: Traditional and modern styles of royal duty.

Europe

Diana's first solo overseas outing was to Monaco. In 1982 she attended the funeral of Princess Grace, reportedly against the wishes of Charles but with the support of the Queen. Ironically, in this respect her first visit was a forerunner of things to come. Charles never seemed able to voice his support for his wife's growing overseas success, unlike the Queen's muted but consistent approval.

Most people probably associate the travelling Princess with humanitarian visits to exotic foreign destinations. And it's true, a photograph of Diana cradling an African baby against a backdrop of dusty rural poverty accurately sums up the value of so much of her charitable work. But the other strand of her public duty was the humdrum business of representing her country or the charities and organisations she represented. The locations were maybe less exotic – and frequently looked downright grey and rainy – but the value of such visits was just as great.

Left: As Patron of the British Deaf Association Diana learnt enough sign language to communicate her feelings, in this case happily acknowledging applause. Opposite: Attending the funeral of Princess Grace of Monaco, 1982.

Opposite: Visiting the Pope, 1985. Above: Grief was no embarrassment for Diana. Her willingness to share others' pain was her most remarkable gift. Bosnia, 1997.

Because the European distances involved were comparatively short – it takes no longer to travel from Kensington Palace to Brussels than to Manchester – most of these visits followed the pattern of a domestic 'away day'. We would leave Kensington Palace at 10.30am sharp, and drive with a police motorcycle escort to Northolt, the RAF base on the western outskirts of London.

On the way I would try to find out what sort of mood my boss was in. Because she generally looked forward to a busy day in a foreign city her mood was usually sunny. But if she was uncommunicative and apparently fascinated by the passing suburban landscape, I knew she was preoccupied. This wouldn't have been surprising given the stress and turbulence of her collapsing marriage, and the public battles with her husband that were the rumbling sub-plot to so much of our work.

But as she climbed the steps into the familiar, cool blue elegance of the royal jet, her natural enthusiasm and professionalism invariably took over. The continuing miracle of Diana in my eyes was not that she was a careworn victim of her predicament – as she was too often happy to portray herself – but that she was a strong, determined woman who refused to let her private unhappiness affect her public performance.

So, as the doors closed, she would settle into her seat and spread out the briefing notes I'd prepared for her on the little wooden folding table. Pausing only to order a camomile tea – and maybe a banana – she would do her homework. For someone with no serious academic qualifications, and who liked to say she was 'as thick as a plank', Diana was surprisingly diligent about paperwork, whether reading my notes or generating her own correspondence. Every afternoon I would send a bag of assorted documents to Kensington Palace for her attention, and every morning without fail it would return with all points dealt with.

In this, as in so much else, she was every inch the conscientious royal professional and not the tearful, self-pitying character she portrayed on tape to shame her in-laws. I always believed that the best response to her

Opposite: Diana's working trips to Europe weren't very glamorous – but they were a vital part of her development as a serious international operator.

'I always believed that the best response to her critics was not tears, but the kind of high-quality public work at which she excelled.'

critics was not tears, but the kind of high-quality public work at which she excelled.

These were my typical thoughts as we'd fly off, and I'm pretty sure they mirrored Diana's. As she methodically scanned her briefing, she would fire questions. What gift did we have for the President? Hadn't the Ambassador's wife just been in hospital? Then send flowers. How long would Diana have in the children's ward of the hospital? Why was I wearing that awful tie? And so on. So long as you had all the answers ready – and a rude retort about the tie – it was great fun. Later she might wander up to the cabin for a chat with her protection officers (the security threat was almost always higher in Europe than at home). And then she'd peer through the open cockpit door and tease the pilots about their duty-free shopping.

Then the engines would throttle back for descent, and through gaps in the clouds straight roads and big square fields would come into view. The Princess usually retreated to the royal powder room for some last-minute DIY on her hair and make-up, while I went to the other loo to check my offensive tie was looking its glorious best.

As the aircraft taxied towards its parking spot next to a line of waiting limousines, tension in the cabin rose to a peak. It always did. Despite all my efforts to calm it, my heartbeat was always accelerating as I peered awkwardly out of the porthole to catch a first glimpse of the press pen and the reception committee. This was usually headed by the reassuring figure of the British Ambassador with the government minister who'd be our host and, next to him, the head of a particular charity and then the security personnel. And there'd be the royal car with the Princess's standard. All present and correct. But I never quite stopped worrying that one day they might be late, have got the date wrong or that we'd land at the wrong airport. Courtiers' mythology was full of such cautionary tales.

The price of survival, certainly in Diana's team, was never to be complacent for a moment. If anything went wrong – even something quite outside my control – the buck would always stop with me. If there was any flaw in the administrative support that underpinned every royal performance, then the Princess would not be seen at her shining best. And second best was never an option.

Persian Gulf

I'd already been working at St James's Palace for about a year before I had a chance to go on a tour. I couldn't wait. Until you'd done an overseas trip, and got the fancy yellow and red label on your briefcase, you weren't really a paid-up member of the team. So the 1989 Gulf Tour marked my graduation from raw apprentice if not to an expert, then at least to a real courtier.

The tour also had a darker significance. It was my first chance to see the Prince and Princess together on the road, and what I saw gave me my first real proof that they remained married in name only. At various revealing moments I observed that they no longer worked as a team, were uncomfortable in each other's company, were distant with each other in public and competed to make a good impression on the press. But they were professionals, doing a job as diplomatic ambassadors for Britain. And – especially on a good day – they were still an unbeatable double act. If you hadn't been on the inside of our travelling circus, you might not even have noticed that they couldn't stand sharing the same spotlight. Nor would you have known that they weren't even sharing the same bedroom.

One of my jobs was to look after the domestic arrangements, and I quickly learned that this included finding polite and discreet ways to ask for 'extra' guest suites at the palaces we stayed in. It wasn't difficult. Our hosts were oil-rich rulers who could have provided a dozen rooms each for their guests and still have plenty to spare. But for me it was depressing confirmation that I was working for a house divided. And I remembered enough scripture to know that a house divided against itself must surely fall… It seemed a suitable quote for our situation, especially against a backdrop of arid desert, palm trees and camels.

The camels gave Diana one of her biggest laughs of the trip in Dubai. Dusk was falling as we took our seats at the floodlit camel race-track. About 20 camels were jostling at the start but, once the race began, the

jostling got even worse. Despite the frantic efforts of the jockeys, some camels obstinately turned around and headed back against the flow of traffic. Others set off at high speed with their riders holding on like grim death.

'How come they don't fall off?' she asked our host. She had a point. No matter how violently the camels manoeuvred, the riders stayed put, as if they were stuck to their saddles. And they *were* stuck to their saddles. After the race Diana was shown the jockeys' secret – thick patches of Velcro tape on the seat of their jodhpurs. The riders (most seemed about seven-years old) laughed as much as she did. After all, it's not every day you get to wave your bum at a Princess.

Next morning, the royal visitors were taken sightseeing in the desert. After a lot of exciting driving up and down steep sand dunes in 4 x 4 cars we stopped for lunch. While we were being scared witless by the jeep drivers, attendants pitched Bedouin tents in a nearby oasis. Deep pits had been dug in the sand, now filled with red-hot charcoal; whole dead lambs went on top, and were covered.

As Charles and Diana took their seats – cross-legged on low cushions – the pits were ceremoniously opened and the lamb produced. It was tender enough to eat with your fingers, which was just as well because that's what we had to do. I anxiously watched Diana to see if she knew about using your right hand for this rather messy task, as custom demands. I needn't have worried. She was a professional Princess, knew enough Arab protocol, and effortlessly made a neat job of it while engaging our host in light conversation. He seemed impressed by her table manners, and even more impressed by her outfit, her 'harem pants' as she called them. But who wouldn't be?

The Princess was due to fly back to London the next day, while the Prince continued to Saudi Arabia. As always, she was very anxious to get home to see 'my boys'. But even she had time to admire the beach palace where she and Charles were staying. It looked as though it belonged in a

Previous spread: Diana loved wearing her 'harem pants' and looked very comfortable sitting on the ground for this Dubai desert picnic. Opposite: Royal duty is traditionally a solemn business – and Diana was never flippant when on duty. But luckily she seldom took it (or herself) too seriously.

'It looked as though it belonged in a James Bond film, an exotic blend of Islamic and modern architecture set against the dazzling turquoise waters of the Persian Gulf.'

James Bond film, an exotic blend of Islamic and modern architecture set against the dazzling turquoise waters of the Persian Gulf. The interior was equally exotic, with gold leaf walls and futuristic furniture mixed with traditional fabrics and air-conditioning.

While the lady-in-waiting and I were being entertained by Diana bouncing on her vast bed, news came that her flight was delayed. During dinner – French not Arabic cuisine this time – we were told it would be seriously late. Sheikh Mohammed immediately came to the rescue, ordering his private jumbo jet to be made ready. So Diana and her companions – I was going to Saudi Arabia with the Prince – flew home from Dubai in what must be the world's ultimate private jet. I went to the airport to take my leave, and heard the Sheikh invite her to help herself in the duty-free shop. It's a famously well-stocked shoppers' paradise, and I could see some of her domestic staff's eyes light up. But Diana, so often unfairly labelled a shopaholic, politely declined the generous offer.

Wise decision, I thought to myself as I bumped back to the palace in an old embassy land rover. Wouldn't the press like to hear about that one. Still, it can't have been easy. Though she wasn't a world-champion shopper, she was as susceptible as anyone to the attractions of material goods. She obviously thought that a few more minutes' conversation with the darkly handsome Sheikh was the right choice. Given the desert that was now her marriage, I didn't blame her one bit.

Opposite page: In 1989 it still seemed possible that Charles and Diana could find a way to stay together – not least for the benefit of official tours like this to Saudi Arabia.

Indonesia and Hong Kong

I don't think I ever went anywhere hotter with Diana than Indonesia. Lying across the equator, the tropical archipelago offered the visiting Prince and Princess a colourful range of engagements to suit their individual styles. But it was *hot*.

The picture that summed up the visit for me was of the Princess sitting under a ceremonial awning at a cultural display. In the midday heat her mascara was beginning to run and she looked very unlike the cool, elegant Princess she normally was. She fanned her face rather limply and, for a moment, I thought she was on the verge of fainting. But she was a trouper. With a visible effort she stuck to her diplomatic duty, and complimented her hosts on the display of local folk dancing. We had a Royal Navy surgeon accompanying us as the tour doctor, but his resuscitating skills weren't needed. The Princess recovered her composure and the doctor lectured us on the dangers of dehydration, especially the kind that followed too many cold beers.

My other main memory is of the Sitanala leprosy hospital. Leprosy was still common in rural Indonesia, and sufferers endured almost medieval levels of suspicion and social exclusion. The authorities were keen to destigmatise the dreaded disease, and Diana was keen to help.

'Don't Do It Di!' warned the newspapers. The Princess ignored them and not only met the patients but sat on their beds and touched them. It was a powerful message of compassion not just to the lepers, but to their families and neighbours. On the world stage, it helped launch the Princess's caring image – an image based on the kind of personal courage and conviction that she showed that day in the tropical heat.

Of course, being Diana, the day wasn't all solemn good works. While touring the leper community she spotted a bowling lawn. In a moment, the patients, medical staff and visitors were playing an impromptu game. And, of course, the Princess joined in, bowling the final ball with uncanny accuracy. It left everybody smiling.

Opposite: In Hong Kong in 1989 Diana was the 'victim' of a friendly ambush by Ghurka army wives who decorated her with traditional garlands.

Top left and right: As well as seeing the deadly serious medical work of the Sitanala leprosy hospital in Indonesia, Diana also took the chance to play an impromptu game of bowls with staff and patients. She never forgot that laughter is the best medicine.
Opposite: Arriving in Hong Kong with Charles, 1989. The Governor's barge *The Lady Maureen* was an elegant setting for this colourful fashion tribute to Chinese style.

It was a typical example of Diana's style of overseas engagement. There were patients to be comforted, staff to be encouraged and British diplomatic interests to be promoted. The inevitable blaze of publicity was beneficial since it helped lift a medical and social stigma, and highlighted a public health message. And it was all done with the professionalism and good humour that were becoming her international hallmark.

Soon the tour party – all 26 of us – was back in our Royal Air Force jet, flying north to Hong Kong. It was Diana's first visit to what was then a British colony, and she found it a very different experience from Indonesia. For one thing, it was a lot cooler. For another, the British Governor was there to meet her and Charles, and take them on his official barge across the spectacular harbour. Finally, there was a royal home-from-home to relax in – the Royal Yacht *Britannia*.

But first she and Charles had to take part in a traditional welcome ceremony. Straight from the Governor's barge, *The Lady Maureen*, they were ushered to a podium in front of several hundred schoolchildren who sang old Chinese greetings, followed by dragon dancers. The blaze of city lights around the spectacular harbour made a dramatic backdrop. Everybody wanted to see what Diana was wearing and, as usual, she did not disappoint. An oriental-style silk hat topped off an exotic mauve and red outfit that shimmered under the spotlights.

Finally, a ceremonial dancing dragon pranced up to the podium and lowered its head respectfully. Diana took a paintbrush and dotted the dragon's eye, as custom required. As the dragon snaked off, the children sang a new song, specially composed for the occasion. The Princess knew these children faced an uncertain future, with Hong Kong due to be handed back to communist China in just a few years. The bright-eyed optimism of their singing made it a poignant moment.

Next day, the Princess set off on a programme of charity engagements which I had set up during my planning visit (or recce) a few weeks earlier. I always tried to make sure that the projects she visited had a link with one

Previous spread: With Indonesian children in traditional dress, Jakarta, 1989.

'This ability to switch in a moment from being "Caring Di" to the cool young future queen was a talent that marked her, in my eyes, as an exceptional royal professional.'

of the organisations of which she was a patron, or concerned something she wanted to learn more about. So we started with the Hong Kong Red Cross. Diana was patron of British Red Cross Youth and, right up to the end of her life, she was a regular supporter of their work. She watched a first-aid lesson which took place – like much of Hong Kong life – in a tower block. The earnest young volunteers were awed by their statuesque blonde visitor. Diana, as usual, set about defusing the tense atmosphere with laughter and smiles, submitting happily to bandage-tying practice and leading the applause at a short awards ceremony.

Later, in a contrast that was typical of the royal working day, Diana visited the Royal Hong Kong Police training school. This was practically a military establishment, staffed by British instructors and was hugely evocative of the colonial era that was coming to an end. Amid the saluting, marching and much stamping of boots, the Princess looked demurely regal.

The change from the laughter of the first-aid lesson could hardly have been greater. But it was typical of her sense of duty that she gave every bit as much attention – and just as many smiles – to a parade of police recruits as she ever gave to a ward of sick children. This ability to switch in a moment from being 'Caring Di' to the cool young future queen was a talent that marked her, in my eyes, as an exceptional royal professional.

Arriving back at *Britannia* I suddenly grew nervous. On the quayside an ambush lurked. It couldn't have been more friendly, comprising the wives and children of Gurkha soldiers waiting to greet her with traditional Nepalese garlands. But it was an ambush nevertheless. It wasn't in the programme. And it lay between the Princess and the bath and rest she badly needed before that evening's official banquet. Sitting next to her in the car I sensed her irritation, and braced myself for the royal rebuke that I was sure must be brewing. She got out of the car as if she'd been looking forward to the moment all day, smiled and chatted as the garlands piled up around her neck, and waved to an enchanted crowd as she then climbed up the gangway.

She was still waving and smiling as I followed her into the staterooms and out of sight. Then, as she took off the garlands, she gave me the rebuke I'd been expecting. Surprises, even nice ones, are not encouraged in royal programmes. But the trace of a smile remained. Although she demanded high standards of herself – and expected her staff to do the same – she knew mistakes sometimes happened. Anyway, I remembered, as a courtier it's your job to take the flak for any mishap, even if it's not your fault. I thought it a small price to pay.

Another highlight of the tour was the Princess's visit to the Helping Hand senior citizens' centre. As patron of Help the Aged and, later, of HelpAge International, she took a close interest in older people's welfare in most countries she visited. This certainly revealed to her the marked variation in how different cultures look after elderly relatives. In China older people are traditionally revered for their wisdom and experience. The Helping Hands centre we saw there lived up to its name, helping its users maintain an independent lifestyle by giving them medical help and lunch, the chance for a good gossip and game of chess. Sometimes the contrast between the grudging attitudes of the 'civilised' West and the developing countries we visited couldn't be greater.

The language barrier might have been insurmountable, but I was already learning that Diana could communicate what she wanted to say very effectively just using her eyes. It still surprises me to hear it said that she was really only interested in children. She did, of course, take a long-term close interest in children's health and wellbeing. But I observed she had her closest rapport with elderly people of all races and cultures. I once asked her about it. 'They've lived through so much, so they're really interesting. You get a lot back from them,' she said. 'Beauty's more than skin deep you know!'

I remembered the point when organising her public charity visits. She was the first to recognise that children, especially sick children, deserved her interest and care. But real involvement was usually only possible with people who could tell her about their experiences. And elderly people, even through an interpreter, could more easily see beyond her celebrity to the vulnerable young woman she knew was the real her. This, in turn, deepened her understanding of the suffering and needs of the people she met on her travels. For her it was a conscious process to help make her better at her job.

The same skill was apparent at another Hong Kong engagement, a visit to a community of recovering drug addicts at Shek Kwu Chau, on an island several miles offshore, in the territory's southern archipelago. The location was breathtaking. As we approached in a helicopter Diana put down her briefing notes and gazed out of the window. The steep-sided island came into view, rising out of the deep blue South China Sea, covered in bamboo and semi-tropical shrubs, like a scene from a willow-pattern plate.

The administrator was a dedicated but rather eccentric expatriate who imposed an enlightened but strict rehabilitation regime on his patients. He believed that removing them from the pressures and temptations of the mainland would speed their recovery, while communal life in unspoilt surroundings would help them overcome the root causes of their addiction.

'Her world of helicopters, royal yachts, limousines, fashion and banquets could be just as isolating as their island.'

Looking around the island it was hard to disagree.

The islanders were almost entirely self-sufficient, each contributing whatever skill they had in the outside world. The Princess declined the offer of a jeep and visited the gardens, workshops, clinic and community hall on foot. Once again the language barrier was easily forgotten: she was patron of a major drugs charity in Britain and knew how to make the addicts feel understood. It's perhaps not often realised that she spent more time on drug and mental health projects than on AIDS, land mines or children's health.

As she was about to leave, the entire community of several hundred gathered to say goodbye. The patients, in simple shorts and T shirts, many wearing home-made sandals, watched with polite curiosity as the exotic figure prepared to return to her infinitely different world. As the helicopter lifted above the tree tops she waved to the little crowd of figures. They waved back. I wondered how many of them could guess that, for a moment, the beautiful Princess with the happy smile wished she could have stayed down there with them.

Her world of helicopters, royal yachts, limousines, fashion and banquets could be just as isolating as their island. And though the patients lived with the prospect of life back on the mainland, for her there would be no return to the world she'd known before she became a princess. It was no surprise that, several years later when she was next in Hong Kong, she asked me to arrange another visit to the place where she had found such tranquillity.

'Nobody noticed when the Princess gently took Mrs Goncz's hand to comfort her. While the men stood solemnly at attention, Diana's simple gesture did more than a hundred anthems to put the seal of friendship on the visit.'

Hungary

In 1990, Hungary was just emerging from communist rule. During the recce we were working with officials who owed their considerable status to the old regime. They seemed distracted by the recent 'velvet revolution', and it was no surprise to find that most of them had been assigned to 'other duties' by the time of the visit. Despite these undercurrents, the visit was a huge success. The summer of 1990 might have been an uncomfortable time to be a communist government official but, for most Hungarians, it was a chance to enjoy new freedoms.

Things got off to a good start at the airport. The Prince and Princess were greeted at the aircraft by President Goncz who, under the old regime, had suffered persecution and imprisonment. Now he personified the new, liberated Hungary. The sun shone. The immaculate guard of honour presented arms for inspection. The band played the national anthems. And the President's wife, overcome with emotion, quietly wept. It seemed that hearing the pre-communist anthem played for the first time in many years had moved her to tears. But nobody noticed when the Princess

Opposite: As the anthems played during the official arrival ceremony, the President's wife was quietly crying with emotion. Nobody noticed… except Diana who un-selfconsciously took her hand in a typically spontaneous gesture.

gently took Mrs Goncz's hand to comfort her. While the men stood solemnly at attention, Diana's simple gesture did more than a hundred anthems to put the seal of friendship on the visit.

The party atmosphere even affected the security arrangements. Our own protection officers asked their Hungarian counterparts to erect crowd-control barriers for the royal walkabouts. The Hungarian police politely declined, explaining that since the collapse of the old regime, citizens of Budapest were now free to stand wherever they liked.

Predictably, excited crowds pressed close to the visitors whenever they could. The Princess, as usual, attracted more than her share. But she operated best in well-controlled surroundings, and quickly grew nervous if hemmed in by admirers, however friendly. Anxious for a snap for the family album, amateur photographers became noisily frustrated while the professional press complained, with good reason, that they weren't able to do their job.

The Hungarian police rapidly realised that our request for crowd control

Above: An impromptu piano recital in Budapest.

was not an attempt to curtail individual freedom, but was a necessary bit of organisation to make sure everybody had a good view. Barriers soon started to appear and our well-practised routine to allow the royal stars to meet their fans worked smoothly again.

The crowds were certainly out in force when Diana visited the Peto Institute. This was the world-famous centre for the treatment of children with cerebral palsy and other disabilities. For thousands of families it is a last refuge of hope when conventional treatments fail. Its therapeutic regime – known as conductive education – had its critics but also a remarkable record of success. The Hungarians were intensely proud of the Peto's pioneering achievements, proof of their enlightened concern for children in desperate need. It was only to be expected that they would want to show it off to the Princess, already a byword for caring celebrity. And it was typical of Diana that she brushed aside the risk of criticism, and seized the chance to highlight a treatment that fulfilled her simple criterion for support: give hope.

So conductive education joined leprosy, HIV/AIDS, mental illness and drug abuse on a growing list of controversial areas that weren't obvious candidates for royal patronage. Diana had an instinct for spotting causes that needed her involvement, regardless of their potential for controversy. And this one repaid her commitment in full. On this first visit, and on a subsequent low-key return trip, the Princess learned at first hand the extraordinary process of teaching severely disabled children how to enjoy a degree of mobility they and their parents had been told would always be beyond them. She also saw for herself the degree of effort, pain and determination that the results demanded. Soon after she got back to England, she accepted patronage of the Institute's British equivalent, the Birmingham Foundation for Conductive Education (now F.C.E.) it too benefited from her long-term support.

The Hungarians were also justifiably keen to show off their beautiful city on the banks of the Danube. But their spiritual home, they explained, was in the countryside, especially on the great Puçta plain where their ancestors had been legendary horsemen. So, in recognition of its symbolic importance, the royal visitors agreed to spend a day on the hot, dusty plain being driven in open carriages, eating goulash and watching folk displays and horsemanship.

I thought it was great fun. And although she was rather preoccupied by some inner worry – and was never very enthusiastic about horses – Diana managed to look happy enough too, especially when the lithe riders performed daring cossack-style stunts for her approval. It was only when we were back in Budapest for the last day of the visit that I realised what was worrying her. Ever since the trip had been announced, some of the Prince's staff had been quietly portraying it as a sign that the royal marriage was not in the dire straits depicted by some of the media. The expression 'second honeymoon' even appeared in one newspaper.

As everybody now knows – and as Diana certainly knew at the time – her marriage was actually in a worse state than even the most doom-laden commentators dared hint at. Pictures of the couple at the famous Fisherman's Bastion beauty spot, or during a boat trip on the romantic Danube, gave the illusion that they were dutifully putting their differences behind them and even smiling at each other. Sadly, it was all a charade.

Diana was rapidly reaching the point where she no longer felt able to play a game that she saw as dishonest. By tradition, a royal wife in her position should have ignored her husband's preference for his mistress, gritted her teeth and done her duty which was to keep up appearances, despite her unhappiness.

The trip she was now on – like all the others with her husband – was a perfect example of that duty. These foreign tours were not holidays, even if they sometimes took her to interesting or exotic destinations. On the contrary: they were integral parts of British diplomatic policy and therefore serious, hard work. But playing the happy wife was taking a terrible toll emotionally, and robbing her of self-respect. 'Patrick, it's so dishonest!' she said to me more and more often. In addition, she was beginning to realise that, given a chance, she could make a big success of representing Britain abroad on her own.

Having seen her grow immeasurably in confidence and poise just in the few trips I'd been on, I knew there was no doubt she could do it. But there was equally little doubt that her husband and his supporters were ambivalent, to say the least, about the idea of a globe-trotting celebrity Princess. Diana's ambition to become a solo royal traveller began to symbolise her dream of breaking free of her dead marriage. After the fake 'second honeymoon' in Hungary, the question was not will the marriage publicly disintegrate, but when.

The last two tours that she and the Prince carried out together proved that sharing the same spotlight had become intolerable for them. At home, behind closed doors, they were already leading lives apart and, on tour, it had become impossible to keep up the pretence of happy normality. During the India tour of 1992, photographs of Diana forlorn in front of the Taj Mahal signalled her determination to end the charade.

Above: Hungary, 1990. Touring together was becoming an unbearable strain on Charles and Diana's marriage.

New York and Washington

Diana made three trips to New York while I was working for her, and then one more before her death. She had a fascination with the city, and the feeling was fully reciprocated. Perhaps each recognised the other as a world-class act, and wondered where the act gave way to reality. The Princess certainly explored New York's glamorous side but, being who she was, also made time to see more of its grittier side than many Manhattan residents might manage in a lifetime.

Her first visit in 1989 set the tone. Arriving at dusk on Concorde, she swept into Manhattan in a 20-car convoy with highly visible, gun-toting secret servicemen. The security threat was real enough, if low-key. Irish Republican protestors tried to disrupt her attendance – as Patron of the Welsh National Opera – at a performance of *Faust* at the Brooklyn Academy of Music. As she left the theatre, police were nervously corralling a noisy group of placard-waving protestors. 'Di Go Home!' wasn't the usual soundtrack to her goodwill missions. Luckily it was never repeated.

More familiar was the cause she supported at the Henry Street Settlement. Set in the deprived inner-city area of the Lower East Side, this was a housing project with a difference. It recognised that social ills must be addressed as a set of inter-related problems. For example, single parenthood – an issue with which Diana felt herself at least slightly acquainted – was a common experience among residents of the settle-ment, and she spent some time talking privately with one young mother.

This was the kind of royal work Diana made her own. Her instinctive gift for putting troubled people at ease and leaving them comforted was the defining quality of her charity work. Lots of people have tried to play up or play down this rare talent, but I suspect only those who have personally experienced it can fully understand its value.

Though our relationship was professional from first to last, during the eight

Opposite: For the New York Fashion Awards in 1994 Diana tried an adventurous slicked-back hairstyle. She was amused by her own daring – and by my startled reaction. 'I know what you're thinking!' she laughed 'This stuff looks like axle grease!'

'Her instinctive gift for putting troubled people at ease and leaving them comforted was the defining quality of her charity work.'

years I worked with Diana there were a couple of occasions when I felt it for myself. Two major family bereavements came my way and I discovered that, almost just by telling her about them, a calm space was made in my confused emotions. It was a safe, neutral place in which pain could be accepted and in which healing might have a chance to begin. I'm not saying she did the healing but she certainly inspired the real hope that it was possible. I saw that belief come to life in sad faces in New York, and all over the world. Looking at some of these pictures, you can see that magical gift still at work today.

Of course, such a gift's true value was in how much it helped the real healers to do their work. Diana knew very well that though fate had given her the job of giving hope, encouragement and maybe even inspiration just by turning up, the real business of caring for those in need was tough, relentless and unglamorous. She may not have done many more good works than anyone else in her brief life. However, on countless occasions, she helped create the circumstances in which good works were possible on a huge scale. That was part of the Princess's magic, too.

The incongruity of the high-born English girl spreading cheerful encouragement to Manhattan's neglected poor takes some beating. But on the last day of that first visit she eclipsed even that success and made a contribution to public health that is now legendary. She went to Harlem Hospital and, while there, picked up and hugged an African-American baby dying of AIDS. AIDS the alleged gay plague. AIDS the new Black Death. AIDS – creator of a whole new caste of untouchables. But until

Above: With Henry Kissinger and Colin Powell at the Humanitarian of the Year Awards, New York, 1995. A special evening for me too – this was to be my last overseas engagement with Diana. Bottom: When in the public eye, even a moment's lapse in concentration could produce a very undiplomatic image. Luckily such mishaps were rare and in this case only the petits fours seemed to have caused offence.

Diana made that gesture the easiest response to AIDS was to ignore it or despise the people who lived with it. Now her involvement helped transform the way in which the disease, and those it touched, were perceived. It helped release funds for research, compassion for the victims and recognition for those dedicated to relieving their suffering.

From then on, whenever she could, Diana made sure I included in her programme engagements that would help lift the stigma of AIDS. In the UK this meant visiting hospitals, hospices, research facilities, day-care centres and public education events. Abroad it took her to African orphanages, and a moving visit to a children's project in Washington DC. I'll come back to this.

The 1989 visit put down the Princess's marker in New York. It established her as an unbeatable combination of fashion and compassion. In the words of a major US charity fundraiser, she had proved she could be 'lightning in a bottle'. But Diana was more than a celebrity with a heart. And I was determined she had to be seen as different. There was no shortage of critics back home who would have been only too happy to see her as nothing more than another insincere cover-girl. Her detractors, I knew, muttered that her version of royal duty seemed to go little further than getting herself photographed in heart-tugging scenes with sick children. 'It's not a popularity contest!' had been one of Prince Philip's truthful, but less than empathetic, bits of advice to her. I knew there was more to Diana, both as a person and as a royal humanitarian symbol, than the critics gave her credit for. The trouble was, I also knew that she had an unfortunate knack of playing into their hands.

In 1993, for example, just when she might have claimed outright moral victory over her enemies with a speech of conciliation and strength, she opted instead for a self-indulgent plea for 'time and space' away from public duties – an emotive and, I knew, insincere grab for sympathy. She repeated the mistake in 1996 with the *Panorama* interview that effectively sealed the fate of her royal career. And mine too.

Previous spread: With George and Barbara Bush at the British Ambassador's Residence in Washington, November 1985. George Bush was Vice President at the time.

Top left and right: The Reagans at the White House, 1985. Bottom left: New York, 1989. The Henry Street Settlement – a housing development where Diana's hands-on style won enthusiastic American approval. Bottom right: With Elizabeth Dole arriving at the US Red Cross Headquarters.

In a minor, but still revealing misjudgement, she seemed to prove her preference for scheming rather than unambiguous good works by getting photographed in a car, secretly briefing the royal correspondent of a newspaper. Even this embarrassment we managed to treat as something of a joke. It was sometimes the best way to get her to listen to criticism. She knew I disapproved, not on moral grounds since her opponents were in no position to preach, but because I felt she needed only to carry on with mainstream charity work and her reputation would look after itself. Her risky attempts to manipulate her image did her no favours, and tied her loyal supporters in knots.

Washington

What no-one could criticise was the kind of 1990 visit to Washington. She went as patron of London City Ballet whose virtuoso performances on stage were not quite being matched in the vital area of fund-raising. That old reliable standby of many a beleaguered royal patronage – the American fund-raising gala – seemed one solution.

These expeditions were generally successful because they involved the British trading what the Americans wanted (royal glitz) for what the fundraisers needed (lots of lovely dollars). Over the decades, the formula had worked over and over again, but some Americans were beginning to tire of what had become nicknamed 'Viking Raids' on their generosity.

Diana offered more than just another begging bowl. Certainly her previous New York visit had had a fund-raising element, but the headlines had been about homelessness and AIDS. Even so, Washington is not New York, as we were discovering. Already there was some scepticism among the Washington social elite: society hostesses were audibly wondering if they really wanted to make room in their packed diaries for this fancy Princess. But with some swift re-jigging of the programme and a minor charm offensive by the ever-helpful British embassy, all was well.

Opposite: Looking regal at the White House.

Top: Diana told me she admired Hillary Clinton's strength. The two women struck up an immediate rapport. Bottom: By the time President and Barbara Bush visited London in 1991 Diana's work for AIDS awareness had been so successful that Mrs Bush chose to accompany her to visit AIDS patients at the Middlesex Hospital. 'For such a powerful lady, she's got great TLC,' Diana told me.

'Washington had allowed itself to be charmed.'

The society queens, having made their point, were generous in their hospitality to the visiting Princess. The fund-raising gala for the ballet company was a highpoint of the Washington calendar, and a local children's AIDS charity received major donations and a very successful royal visit.

So did the President and Mrs Bush. Since Barbara Bush was another campaigner for AIDS charities, she and Diana had a lot to discuss on the subject, not to mention spaniels and the décor of the White House. She had slightly less to discuss with President Bush (Snr) on the subject of the Gulf War, which was then imminent, so instead she flirted with him. It was not her best-ever performance, but it still managed to combine regal dignity with sparkling eye contact and laughter. It seemed to do the trick. A few days later a letter typed by the President himself was received requesting a photograph for the family.

As we flew home at supersonic speed, Diana opened her briefcase and we got started on thank you letters. Some she did in her own hand, most were for me to finish in the office on her behalf. She had good reason to be pleased: after initial resistance, Washington had allowed itself to be charmed. Her ballet patronage had raised the necessary funds. The AIDS charity, Grandma's House, had also received essential funding and a useful publicity boost. Best of all – to me at least – the White House visit had showed once again that Diana could be a welcome royal visitor with presidents, just as she could with orphans and ballerinas. Which was just as well because that year was her toughest one yet on the home front.

In 1990 the Princess was in a private and public dilemma. In public, she was being portrayed by a sentimental media as a devoted wife attending her husband in hospital where he was being treated for a polo injury. In private, however, she knew that the real nursing effort was being supplied by Camilla Parker-Bowles.

Apart from her children, Diana had no alternative source of comfort in her life. None of her attempts at affairs gave her the long-term affection her husband had secured. Her public life, therefore, increasingly became the stage on which her inner unhappiness was acted out. The emotion she might have confined – in the royal way – to life behind palace doors she instead poured into her work.

In the end, burning precious emotional reserves to propel her public image cost her dear. Arguably, it cost her life. But, in the short term, the results were almost entirely for the good, especially for those lucky enough to meet her and feel the warmth of her interest and concern.

However, from my standpoint, as the chap trying to produce a reliable royal road show, the overall effect could be a bit patchy. 'Stand-by for a mood swing, boys!' she would warn me and the Personal Protection Officer with a giggle. We all dutifully smiled, but the smile became more of an effort as it became apparent that her moods could go down as well as up.

But that was OK. We knew working so closely with such a popular but complex personality would sometimes be challenging at a humdrum, face-to-face level. So if there were days when she was less 'Caring Di' than 'Snappy, Unreasonable, Unfair and a bit Sneaky Di' then so be it. There might be weeks when the laughs didn't outnumber the grumps yet we, who went on the road with her, were better placed than anyone to see the hope and happiness she spread wherever she went.

In other words, she was easy to forgive. Anybody with such an ability not only to admit their own weaknesses but laugh at them deserved a margin for moodiness. That forgiveability was always her ace card, and the world was happy for her to play it over and over again. She was worth it.

Opposite: Diana with her Humanitarian of the Year Award, New York, 1995. Usually she declined such recognition, believing her job was to give awards not receive them. For Henry Kissinger and Colin Powell, however, she made an exception.

PART 2 AMBASSADOR AT LARGE

'She was undoubtedly one of the best ambassadors for Great Britain.'
Nelson Mandela

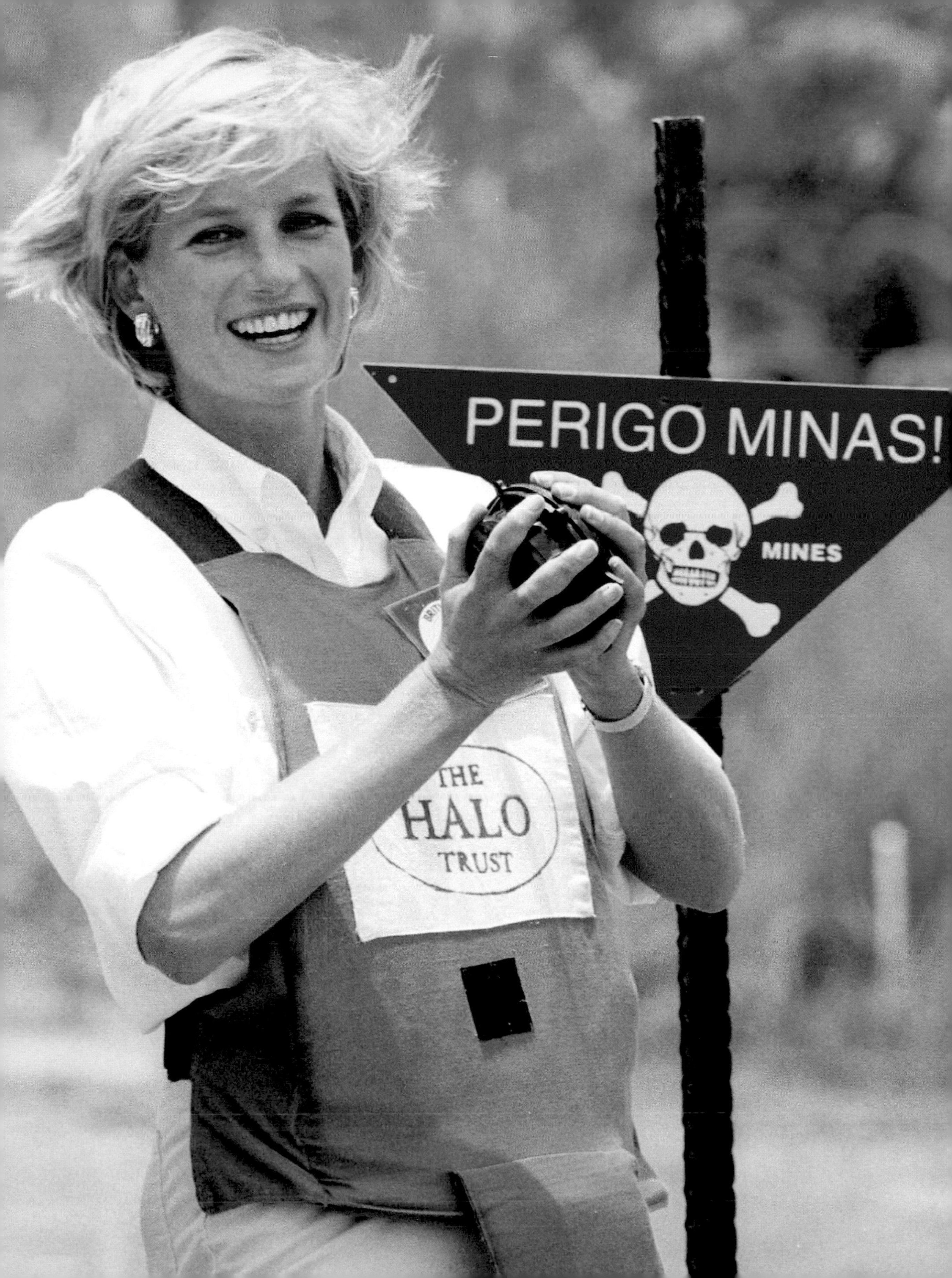
PERIGO MINAS!
MINES
THE
HALO
TRUST

Pakistan

Diana took all her overseas visits very seriously, not just because they were vital to the development of her own status but because she thoroughly understood the importance of being a good ambassador for Britain, and the charities and organisations she was supporting.

Pakistan was Diana's first major solo tour, a make-or-break mission. Any hopes she had of becoming an independent royal operator depended on her making a success of the most demanding overseas tour she had ever attempted. The gamble paid off triumphantly: 'The Princess took Pakistan by storm' reported the High Commissioner to the Foreign Secretary. This success cleared the way for her to begin her career in earnest as a world-wide force for good. But it nearly didn't come off.

The omens had not been good. The trip had originally been scheduled for 1990, and I had optimistically flown to Pakistan and conducted a painstaking planning-visit. This had taken me from the President's office in Islamabad to health projects in the tropical streets of Lahore, and even into the remote splendour of the Khyber Pass. Neighbouring Afghanistan was in the throes of another civil conflict, and during the recce we took time to examine the ruins of a building recently hit by a Scud missile.

But while I was busy organising all the preparations for a royal visit – everything from motorcades to protocol, press and security arrangements – not forgetting the exact spot where posies of flowers were to be presented – Pakistan had been experiencing its own internal disruption. When we returned to the High Commissioner's stylishly modern residence, we found the diplomatic quarter surrounded by a ring of armoured vehicles. There had been a coup in which Mrs Bhutto, the Prime Minister and the Princess's host, had been unceremoniously deposed.

The sudden change of government may or may not have been good for Pakistan, but it undoubtedly put a big question mark over prospects for the royal visit. The British Foreign Office regarded the Princess as a glamorous

Opposite: Pakistan, 1996. Diana never lost her knack with babies – though this one seems less convinced!

and highly effective player on the international, diplomatic chess board, like other members of the Royal Family. But because they all held a unique position as non-political goodwill ambassadors, it was essential that wherever possible they were never put in a position where they were drawn into a host country's internal political squabbles.

Given the Princess's well-publicised similarities with Mrs Bhutto – both were seen as glamorous, influential and independent women (they even famously shared the same London hairdresser at the time) – I knew that the chances of the Foreign Secretary allowing the trip to go ahead as planned were slim. Sure enough, I was still in the baggage hall at Gatwick on returning from my recce when I was called with the news that the Pakistan tour was cancelled.

This was a huge disappointment. Even worse – it meant that Diana had lost an opportunity to show off her paces as an independent royal traveller in her own right. Since she and the Prince were stuck in the mire of a very public and acrimonious separation, the cancellation was a double blow. She had badly needed this trip to reinforce her position at the centre of the royal firm, at a time when there was no shortage of people ready to raise questions about her suitability to be in it at all.

Even so, as things turned out, the year's delay that now followed was perhaps not a bad thing. The Princess used it to build up the bedrock of her home support with a full programme of public duties covering the whole spectrum, from state occasions to the wholesome day-to-day routine of charity project visits and fund-raising.

She and the Prince endured another year of public wrangling and, at the end of it, she emerged strengthened – not just in public affection but, crucially, in her own self-belief. So, when the tour was eventually re-instated in 1991, she was in a far better state to give it her best shot. For that matter, so was her organisation. I made another recce to Pakistan to make quite sure nobody had moved the Khyber pass, and was accompanied by the Princess's press secretary and protection officer. We reviewed the

Right: Pakistan tour, 1991.

Above: In the Red Mosque at Lahore, 1991. Diana was careful to observe Muslim dress conventions. In the background, even the Private Secretary's socks are on view!

plans we had drawn up the previous year, and made a few significant improvements.

For our hosts, the reinstated visit was a welcome sign of international approval for the new regime. So when I gave the Princess the final version of her draft programme, I knew we'd put the year's delay to very good use.

From this time on she made a point of getting to know the Foreign Secretary of the government of the day. This was a shrewd move. Not only did she develop strong relations with them on a personal level, but also earned their support when they saw that she could be trusted to do a good job. In all her years as a royal tourist, Diana never drew a word of criticism from her hosts; she never committed any diplomatic blunders or gaffes. In fact, she earned enormous amounts of goodwill wherever she went. Even towards the end of my time with her, when her status as a separated wife created some doubt about protocol, her hosts – including

Above: Diana and Mother Teresa met on several occasions. Though poles apart in age, experience and vocation, each recognised the power the other had to do good. It created an unusual bond between them.

120

'In all her years as a royal tourist, Diana never drew a word of criticism from her hosts; she never committed any diplomatic blunders or gaffes.'

prime ministers, presidents and the Emperor of Japan – were in no doubt about her world-class stature as a campaigner for good causes.

The Foreign Secretary at the time of the Pakistan trip, and for most of Diana's overseas tours, was Douglas (now Lord) Hurd. We always made sure that he was well briefed on the Princess's hopes and plans for future royal visits and, in turn, he quickly came to value what a popular international representative she could be.

For Pakistan, as for all the Muslim countries she visited, Diana was acutely aware of local sensitivities regarding the status of women. She always made sure she had a suitable scarf to cover her hair when visiting mosques, and her hemline visibly dropped. In Pakistan she made a particular point of wearing green, the colour of Islam and of the Pakistani flag. I also happened to think it rather suited her.

Although the Princess generally took a small retinue of personal staff on these tours, for a major tour like this I knew she had to have all the support necessary for her to give the star performance that was expected.

The Pakistan touring party was fairly typical. One of the most important people on the list was the lady-in-waiting. This was an old-fashioned name for an old-fashioned job. All female members of the Royal Family employ a lady-in-waiting – most employ enough to field a five-a-side football team. The LIWs (as they are called) are usually part-timers, but a few are permanent members of the royal household, organised in a rotating duty roster. This means that neither the LIW nor the royal employer has to put up with the other for more than a week at a time.

The Princess employed between five and seven LIWs during my time. Their duties were undefined but generally consisted of acting as her official, unpaid companion. They were also responsible for helping collect flowers on walkabouts, and carrying a spare pair of tights – and other mysteries – in their handbags. Despite this, their function was primarily traditional and decorative.

When the going got tough, as when Diana started to visit street sleepers, battered wives and secure hospitals, it was possible to think of the LIW, rather unkindly, as unnecessary ballast in the royal showboat. The Princess sometimes even became resentful of their well-meaning attempts at companionable but inconsequential chat.

Nevertheless, I found that a confident LIW who was well-briefed and alert to the Princess's current preoccupations could help smooth over many rocky passages in a day of official engagements. Also I found them, without exception, to be kind, resourceful and fun even when they were first in line for any of our boss's glummer moods. This included contributing to the bad-taste witticisms, impersonations, practical jokes and general ribaldry which seemed to play such a large part in maintaining royal morale on the road.

Right: On a private visit to Pakistan, 1997.

India

Previous spread: A fateful shot. As Diana knew it would, this picture more than any words tells the world that her marriage has become a lonely sham. Opposite: The India tour of 1992 provided timeless images of East and West.

Korea

By the time of the ill-fated South Korea tour of 1992, the Charles–Diana situation had reached meltdown. Images of the couple looking sullen robbed the tour of any diplomatic benefit. A last-minute appeal for press restraint fell on deaf ears and, as the Prince and Princess returned separately to London, it was clear that the marriage had only weeks to live.

Above: The Korean tour of 1992 was the Waleses' last together. Pictures like this told the story plainly enough, even if we were still trying to deny it. Opposite: Despite the gloomy looks of the Korean tour and the news of Charles and Diana's formal separation which followed, just a few months later they were able to appear again in public and play their role as true royal professionals (Liverpool Battle of the Atlantic service, 1992).

'Her inner strength and determination to do her duty as she saw it, shines all the more heroically because — as she was usually quick to admit — she was not perfect.'

Cairo

If Diana at the Taj Mahal had been a plea for sympathy, Diana at the pyramids was a dramatic assertion of independence and strength. Ironically, on the plane to Cairo she had been reduced to tears as her husband — who had shared the plane as far as Ankara — got off to enjoy a private holiday in Turkey.

But, showing a strength which always wrong-footed her critics, Diana dried her eyes, put on fresh make-up and descended on Cairo like a royal trouper. Her inner strength and determination to do her duty as she saw it, shines all the more heroically because — as she was usually quick to admit — she was not perfect. So it's with no disrespect that I sometimes mention her all-too human failings. Without them, her strengths would lack much of their lustre.

It was dark when we arrived in Egypt. But as soon as the corporal opened the door of the Queen's Flight jet a warm blast of scented desert air wafted into the cabin. Inside, Diana waited in the cramped vestibule, out of sight of the reception committee gathered at the foot of the steps but tense, like an athlete waiting for the starting pistol. The lady-in-waiting and I crowded behind her and, as usual, the Princess lightened the tension with some very unroyal humour. Part of the routine was to intersperse the jokes

Right: Even the solemnity of the Commonwealth War Cemetery in Cairo could be momentarily interrupted by a playful breeze.

with quick-fire questions to me about the Ambassador's first name, the number of people in the line-up, the points for discussion in the obligatory arrival photo-call and a host of similar details. She kept you on your toes.

The Queen's Flight Commodore – immaculate tropical uniform ironed to perfection – pushed past to take his place at the foot of the aircraft steps, usually with another royal witticism in his ears ('You might at least have had your jacket pressed!' was the kind of thing). Down below, soldiers were unrolling the last few feet of red carpet up to the steps.

At last the protection officer was satisfied with arrangements on the tarmac and nodded to the Princess. 'Everybody ready?' she called over her shoulder. 'Too late if you're not!' and with that she was off. The lady-in-waiting and I held back for a moment so that the world's first sight of Diana in Egypt was unencumbered by hangers on. (We always tried to give her plenty of elbow room. I've never overcome my suspicion of aides who get themselves into the same camera shot as their boss. There was only ever one star in our show.) The dark cabin was suddenly bathed in the lurid blue light of a score of flashbulbs. As the flashing died away we made our move, and followed the Princess out of the door and into the controlled bedlam down on the apron. Once again, it was curtain up for The Diana Show.

At the bottom of the steps the Ambassador was presenting a minister, a distinguished lady with responsibility for family policy (a major portfolio in a country with an exploding birth-rate). A line of respectful handshakes followed, accompanied by bows and curtsies from the Brits and beaming smiles from the Egyptians. Anxious press and security officials flitted about, some walking comically backwards along the red carpet ahead of the advancing guest. Finally, there were girls with flowers. The flashbulbs blazed again.

I quickly ducked under the wing to check that our baggage was being safely unloaded. It sometimes seemed I spent more time worrying about baggage arrangements and staff transport than about whether the Princess

Above: The 1992 tour of Egypt was another triumph for Diana – and gave the photographers an exciting range of backdrops. The Temple at Karnak is a powerful symbol of Egypt's pride in its antiquities and Diana's visit was a mixture of diplomatic courtesy and sightseeing.

Top: Diana also excelled at mainstream, traditional royal work. The Commonwealth War Cemetery, Heliopolis, Egypt. Bottom: Time off to relax. Wherever she was in the world, Diana always tried to fit in an early morning swim.

was being kidnapped. Any sensible private secretary made sure the accompanying domestic staff – the dresser, butler, cook, hairdresser and yeoman – were also being looked after like a special brand of royalty. Which, of course, they were.

After the customary formal welcome chat in an icily air-conditioned VIP lounge, the Princess climbed elegantly into her armour-plated limousine and set off through Cairo's suburbs to the British Embassy. The embassy pick-up with the luggage had its own escort and, if all went to plan, would reach the Ambassador's residence well before the Princess.

This might seem a mundane detail, but hard experience had taught me the importance of getting the domestic arrangements absolutely right. The domestic staff had the task of delivering the Princess each morning bright and ready for the engagements I inflicted on her. This meant they had to create a little bit of home for her, however unfamiliar our temporary quarters. They had to be good at anticipating her requirements, and untiring in carrying them out. It helped if they could also avoid being unduly distracted either by Diana's frequent praise or her occasionally sharp criticism.

All of us who worked for Diana knew that an unwritten part of our duties was to absorb her occasionally volatile changes of mood. I'm sure this is true of anyone who works closely with a big star. I'm equally sure that Diana was far more modest and considerate to her staff than you'd imagine, given her dizzy ascent to becoming the world's most famous woman.

She was quick to notice particularly good work. But, having many of the qualities of a born leader, she also had a sharp eye for shortcomings. It was a mistake to underestimate her, as her critics discovered to their cost. Taking a lead from Charles – who was famously particular about his creature comforts – Diana expected a high standard from her support team wherever we were in the world. Given the intense scrutiny she was under every time she appeared in public, this wasn't an unreasonable demand. She didn't spare herself when on duty, and didn't expect any less of the people on her payroll.

Zimbabwe

It sometimes comes as a surprise to learn that the British Royal Family has no supreme co-ordinator who oversees everyone's movements to ensure a coherent and efficient use of these expensive assets.

Every so often an attempt is made to impose direction from the centre. Nevertheless, even recent initiatives to apply such elementary good management have had only limited success. The truth is, the Royal Family's organisational unity resembles a solar system of federated but independent planets, revolving around the monarch who is the ultimate source of energy without which they cannot operate.

As in many federations, the constituent members guard their independence jealously. The British royal federation is no exception – not surprising if you consider that a royal person's raison d'être is, by definition, to be above the rules that apply to mere subjects.

Diana's position after separation from Prince Charles caused problems for this ramshackle but well-established system. To suspicious observers on other royal planets she was a new and potentially dangerous heavenly body on an unstable orbit. Nobody knew where she might fly off to next, and most thought the safest reaction was to keep their distance. Knowing this, I took extra care to present the Princess's overseas travel ambitions as just another variation on the traditional royal theme. Federations may be unwieldy, but they do have the advantage of accommodating wide variations in individual style.

So I developed close links with the Royal Matters Section of the Foreign Office. This small department compensated for many of the Royal Family's organisational shortcomings by overseeing the various royal itineraries. It also gave invaluable advice on how to respond to invitations to visit particular foreign countries.

The rules of the game were that it could not instruct a royal person to carry out an overseas engagement, and it could not forbid it. It could only advise

Top left: Diana in Africa, 1991. In support are the Personal Protection Officer (PPO) Ken Wharfe (left) and Press Secretary Dickie Arbiter (right, in glasses). Top right: In 1993 Robert Mugabe had yet to acquire his later notoriety. Bottom: The photographers loved this one...

'She makes you feel good!'

and warn. But the wise private secretary also tried to make sure that his or her royal boss wasn't at odds with government thinking – at least publicly – and that his boss wasn't at odds with another member of the Royal Family. Every few months the private secretaries would gather around a big table in the Buckingham Palace billiard room to share the limited amount of information we felt it necessary to disclose to our colleagues. This included our overseas travel plans which, with the help of the official from the Royal Matters Section, we would then disentangle, if necessary.

One person Diana avoided tangling with was the Princess Royal, Princess Anne. At its warmest, their relationship was one of professional royal operators who admired each other's results, even if their methods were very different. As Patron of the Save the Children Fund, the Princess Royal was seen in royal circles as having laid claim, in a charitable sense, to the continent of Africa. This didn't mean that her male relatives and even, occasionally, the Queen didn't also visit African countries, but their activities could seldom be seen as any kind of competition.

That could hardly be said of plans by Diana to visit what was seen as Princess Anne's turf. But such a visit was probably overdue. Several of Diana's charities ran major aid and development programmes in Zimbabwe, and when a group of them got together to propose a joint programme of engagements it was obviously time to resolve the issue of whether Africa was big enough for both princesses.

Of course it was. When she had plucked up courage – which didn't take long – Diana was quite capable of cutting through palace red tape by picking up the phone and sorting things out with another member of the Royal Family. On one memorable occasion she even got a reluctant Prince Charles to phone the Queen in the middle of a programme-planning meeting. The result was a quick and easy solution to a tricky diary problem. Bypassing normal administrative channels in this way could save huge amounts of time and effort. Which may be why nobody did it very often.

On this occasion, the direct approach worked quite happily. The royal sisters-in-law agreed they wouldn't be stepping on each other's toes; the Foreign Office was enthusiastic, and the Queen conveyed her approval. Planning for the trip moved into top gear. I did another enjoyable recce.

The Zimbabwe tour marked another important milestone in the development of Diana's overseas campaigns. Up to now, I had acted as the central co-ordinator of the various charity programmes proposed for a foreign visit. This could be quite complicated as we'd thrash out priorities, logistics, travel constraints and generally agree a set of compromises to make the best use of limited time. For this trip, however, the three charities concerned – the Red Cross, Help the Aged and the Leprosy Mission – worked as a team to agree their own priorities. The system worked very well and had the added advantage that the heads of each organisation, who by now were familiar, friendly faces, together accompanied their patron for most of the tour.

All this still had to be dovetailed with the High Commission's requirements, and agreed by the host government. Finally it had to be written up by me as an attractive narrative in which the Princess could picture herself step-by-step from leaving Kensington Palace to returning one week later.

As with any trip, I gave the Princess a thorough briefing on what she could expect – the climate, local customs, diplomatic and political sensitivities, the work of the projects and charities she would visit, the importance of commercial ties that she was strengthening, and a thousand other details. For light relief I added some semi-scurrilous and hopefully entertaining pen portraits of the main players she would meet. I also showed her photographs.

I made sure that the Queen had a suitably expurgated version of the same document. It was important to Diana that Her Majesty knew what she would be doing when she was abroad representing Britain, and in turn the Queen always gave Diana encouragement and support in her overseas work. Sometimes, though, Diana felt she could have done with more clearly expressed support. Secretly, I knew she yearned for it. But because of the overheated internal palace politics of the time, the Queen had to be seen to be even-handed between the Princess and Charles. That was never going to be easy. Nor was it always the Queen's way to express her encouragement and guidance in ways that Diana found easy to recognise. That led to some avoidable unhappiness.

The narrative that I had prepared also gave the Princess a chance to fine-tune her wardrobe. For example, she was careful not to wear colours that might cause offence to local religious sensitivities or even to football teams. For official visits (i.e. those undertaken at the request of the government), she was given a dress allowance which, over the years, amounted to several hundred thousand pounds. Though the expense startled me at first, I soon realised that being a mobile shop window for British fashion talent was an expensive business. It was also a shrewd commercial investment on behalf of the fashion industry. And nobody could deny she gave good value for money.

Though, by royal standards, Diana later became a byword for travelling light, in the early days her clothing and accompanying accessories could comfortably fill a commercial van. By the time of my last few tours her travelling luggage required only a station wagon, and on our short European trips she made a point of carrying all her own overnight kit in an elegant leather holdall. So much for her reputation as a clothes addict.

Finally, the narrative gave me a chance to warn her of anything which might annoy or surprise her, which was often the same thing. Lots could come under this heading, but the key was to spell out clearly anything that might catch her unawares when she was in the public eye. It was common sense really, and her tolerance levels grew as her experience and confidence accumulated.

The most important potential problems were major changes to her routine, such as having to start earlier than our usual time of 10am, or undertake a particularly gruelling sequence of engagements, such as an orphanage followed by a hospital followed by a banquet and then a speech.

Incidentally, the 10am start was not because she was a late riser, far from it. But she knew that when she got into her car to go to the first engagement of the day she triggered the start of a complex interconnected sequence of events. This might involve caterers, sniffer dogs, florists, journalists and air-traffic controllers, not to mention her dressers and hairstylist.

The chances of all this machinery working efficiently and happily were hugely increased if the Princess at the centre of it all pressed the Go button at a civilised hour. Experience had shown that 10am suited everybody fine.

In giving my pre-tour briefing to Diana, it was also a good idea to spot any potentially unflattering camera angles. Ladders or exposed windy platforms might require lead weights in the hem of her skirt, or even a switch into flattering chinos. Achieving that perfect look in front of the lens often took a lot of forethought.

This was also the place to warn about what types of food to expect, and potentially tricky or entertaining personalities. On most visits, even working ones, the head of government would invite Diana to call. The Foreign Office always provided guidance notes to help the flow of conversation at what could be rather stilted occasions. These often contained warnings of subjects to avoid. In one instance, the president's family had recently had an embarrassing experience involving the use of illegal drugs. The Princess had to remember not to talk about one of the rehabilitation projects she was visiting as they made light conversation in front of the cameras. In the event, the poor chap seemed so mesmerised by her smile – and other physical attributes – that she could have recited her laundry list for all he cared.

Diana, as Britain's sexiest diplomat, wasn't a proposition that we openly discussed. Her ability to charm the pants (metaphorically) off almost any-

Opposite: Zimbabwe, 1993. Diana lends a hand at a Red Cross feeding station. I was uneasy about this rather contrived shot – and so, I knew, was Diana. Although it made a great picture, it looked too much like a staged stunt. The African boy apparently begging for food was demeaning – and an emotive misrepresentation of the truth. Diana didn't need such tricks to get her message across.

'For somebody universally admired for her beauty, she could be surprisingly vulnerable to attacks of doubt about her real attractiveness.'

body was just one of those things we took for granted. Provided you chose your moment – and your words – carefully, it certainly never did any harm to remind her of this talent. For somebody universally admired for her beauty, she could be surprisingly vulnerable to attacks of doubt about her real attractiveness.

Nevertheless, her attractiveness was a powerful unspoken element in her value as a national representative. 'She makes you feel good!' was Robert Mugabe's enthusiastic verdict, and nobody thought that he meant that she made him feel virtuous. Another leader – a square-jawed pilot and owner of dark flashing eyes – repaid her sex appeal in kind. As the Ambassador and I watched the President and Princess flirt to the limit of diplomatic courtesy, the minutes ticked away. Soon we were running late. This could have had a serious knock-on effect on our schedule.

I fixed a 'let's get moving' stare on Diana, but she refused to acknowledge it. The Ambassador coughed significantly. Still they chatted away. He coughed again, and was ignored again. Just when I thought His Excellency was about to expire, a more decisive presidential aide politely but firmly reminded the VIPs that they each had important engagements for which they had to leave. 'Straight away, please.' 'That was lucky,' said the Ambassador to me quietly as we left the presidential palace. 'I thought we were going to have to throw a bucket of water over them!'

These photographs convey a sense of the excitement that surrounded Diana in Zimbabwe. The friendly exuberance of the people, the beauty of

Opposite: Diana was Patron of British Red Cross Youth but her involvement with the wider Red Cross movement took her all over the world.

146

their country and the dignity of the charity work she saw, all contributed to the feeling that this was her best trip yet.

But far away from the cameras I saw another side of the Princess. It was sometimes possible to suspect that her caring image was just that – an image put on for public consumption. Very occasionally I knew there was some truth in that. Diana would hardly have been human if she hadn't sometimes had partly to feign the concern that was expected of her, especially given the pressures and tensions of her private life.

Yet what was so remarkable about her charity work – and what eventually took its toll on her – was her willingness to expose her own emotions when communicating with sufferers. It may have cost her dear in the long run, but it undoubtedly gave her words of comfort the ring of authenticity. It was a sacrifice she made over and over again, and it stood in clear contrast to the reserved style of traditional royal practice.

For example, one evening in Harare the Princess was visiting an orphanage for children whose parents had died of AIDS. Their mothers and fathers were members of a whole generation of adults in the prime of life who had been decimated by the disease. These orphans were carrying the consequences: none of them would survive into adolescence.

The nurses were mother, father and family to them and Diana watched as, by the light of flickering lanterns, they put the children to bed. As the small figures knelt to say their prayers, the Princess turned away. But not before I'd seen the tears on her cheeks.

Angola

Above: Angola, 1996 – an iconic image of Diana and landmine victims.

Diana's support for the anti-landmines campaign was her last major humanitarian involvement.

Nepal

Diana's visit to Nepal was special for a number of reasons. First, the country itself. The Himalayan kingdom is home to some of the most fabulous scenery and extreme poverty in the world. Both offered huge scope for the kind of picture-friendly tour that was now Diana's hallmark.

And then there was the involvement of a government minister. Lynda Chalker, generally considered an extremely popular and effective Minister for Overseas Development, had also taken unusual care to understand both sides in the 'War of the Waleses'. This was the media's name for the slow public disintegration of Charles and Diana's marriage and the open acrimony that accompanied it.

That war (sometimes the word *war* seemed an understatement) was at its peak at the time of the Nepal tour and I was glad to think that, via Lynda Chalker, accurate reports of the Princess's value as a royal ambassador would reach the Prime Minister. Though she could not expect any senior politician publicly to take her side in the marital conflict, at least her husband's protagonists wouldn't have the field all to themselves.

Diana needed all the powerful friends she could get. In the wake of the *annus horribilis* of 1992, the Queen had ruled that she no longer wanted Diana to represent her abroad. This constraint may not have been spelt out in detail but, whatever position you took, it was hardly a ringing endorsement of our work. Moreover, in the fight to preserve Diana's royal status and safeguard her role as patron of a hundred good causes, she was under attack from critics in the Prince's camp. Since these included at least one government MP, the chance to prove her worth in the expert, unbiased eyes of Lynda Chalker was a valuable opportunity.

The final element of the Nepal tour that made it special to me was that my first daughter was expected to be born a few days before we were due to set out. I was reasonably confident of a sympathetic attitude from the Princess on such an important personal matter – she was, after all, patron of the mother and baby charity Birthright (now Wellbeing) – but I was under no illusion that the royal machine would stop just to suit my convenience.

Still, I thought it prudent to prepare for the tour on the basis that I might not actually be making the trip. Loyal servant I might be; but being absent for such an important event was a sacrifice I wasn't going to ask my family to make. There had already been far too many and I suspected – rightly – that there were many more to come.

Diana agreed to spare me if need be, though not without some resistance. This wasn't so much a reflection of my indispensability – nobody is indispensable in royal service – so much as a recognition that her performance as an independent royal operator was under the micro-scope. She knew that my experience would be more use to her in Kathmandu than in the delivery room of the Chelsea and Westminster Hospital. We agreed to keep the subject under review. The stork might be early.

This was the background for my pre-tour planning trip. When I had joined the household I had been sceptical about the word 'recce'; perhaps, as some of the office staff suspected, they were just jaunts in the sun. I imagined it was just used because of the preponderance of army officers in the palace. As a navy man, I was sure they'd got it wrong. But I soon realised they were, if anything, making light of it. The reality of these planning trips was every bit as painstaking as a military operation. 'Time spent in reconnaissance is seldom wasted,' said the Duke of Wellington. He might have been speaking about the Peninsular War, but his words applied just as much to our planning tours. They were like military operations. We had to prepare for anything that might be thrown at us.

Accompanied by the head of the Princess's security detail, the press secretary and a Commodore of the Queen's Flight, I set off for the Himalayan kingdom to spy out the land, survey all the important objectives, recruit allies and locate any potential booby traps. Transport and communications had to be organised as well as accommodation, food and supplies for the troops.

Considering these recces have been made for decades, I was surprised when I joined the Household not to find a handy little book of guidance which would tell me what to do. True, there were a few notes about domestic requirements. For example, I had to make sure that the Princess's dresser had a free-standing hanging rail, a table to iron on, her own cleaning materials, so many towels, a well-lit mirror, etc., etc. But nowhere could I find anything like a step-by-step guide to the perfect royal tour. No such guide existed, at least for the Waleses. So we made it up as we went along. This may have been a positive advantage since it meant we approached each new expedition with an open mind. There was little chance to settle into a deadening routine of time-honoured rules — we were too busy re-inventing the wheel.

This attitude seemed to suit both the Prince and the Princess who had a reputation for innovation, unlike the predictability of the long-established Buckingham Palace approach. Traditionally, the heir has latitude to evolve new styles. The Waleses were younger and less formal than the Queen and — at least on the surface — displayed a closer personal involvement in the people they met and the causes they supported.

After Charles and Diana separated, the innovation stopped being just a matter of individual royal style. For Diana, it became a professional necessity. A consequence of her new independent royal path was that someone — mostly me — had to develop new ways of building it, and of explaining to sceptical bystanders what we were doing. Nor did we have the luxury of a nice, safe development period in which to practice. Under the unremitting glare of the world's media, not to mention a watchful royal establishment back home, we had to get it right first time.

Our motto was 'Make It Work' and not 'Make It The Way It's Always Been'. 'Make it Happy' was almost as important, and 'Make it Royal' was, thanks to the Princess's instinctive nobility, a foregone conclusion.

These three priorities made a pretty good mission statement for a Diana tour. I might have added 'Make It Quick' because Diana hated missing weekend visits to William and Harry's boarding school. And 'Make It Look Good In The Newspapers' was equally crucial. But I quickly learned that if we got all the other requirements right, a good press report would automatically follow. It was only when we tried to spin the news to make a bad tour look good – a medicine still prescribed by some royal spin doctors – that things went wrong, the disastrous Korea tour of 1992 being the best example, as Dickie Arbiter describes on page 210.

All these thoughts were in the back of my mind as our little recce party flew via India to Nepal. Flying, even as a passenger, was a passion that royal service allowed me to enjoy frequently. I never tired of it, unlike Diana for whom it was a necessary chore. She called the vintage red Queen's Flight Wessex helicopter 'The Flying Tumble Drier'. And if there was turbulence, a technical delay or a tediously long overnight flight she would tease me by telling everyone else that at least Patrick was having fun.

Approaching Kathmandu airport through the towering Himalayas was certainly a thrill. But that was tempered because we were due to plan a visit by Diana to the memorial for passengers lost in an airliner that had recently hit one of the peaks I was at that very moment admiring out of the window. That evening we had dinner with the British Ambassador and his staff. We outlined our proposals. They listened politely and then gently told us why some of them wouldn't work. Then they told us how to make them better.

We had dozens of meetings like this, in embassies all over the world. Without our embassies hardly any royal overseas tours would happen, and any success those tours achieve is largely thanks to our diplomats. We descended on them with our often eccentric or unrealistic ideas, disrupted their routines, made endless calls on their skill, tact and hospitality, and then flew away again leaving a mountain of hard work behind.

Opposite: The ancient Himalayan kingdom of Nepal gave Diana a particularly warm welcome.

Instead of greeting us with snarls they were unfailingly polite, and even let us believe that we were giving their work a boost. It suited me to believe them of course, though I also remembered the old joke that a diplomat is a person sent abroad to lie for his country. If they lied to us, I can only say they did it very convincingly.

By now I had a clear mental picture of what our recces were trying to achieve. That picture only came to me after a lot of trial and error, but it was worth the effort. Once you knew what your boss wanted and what would work, you encountered one of the peculiarities of being a royal private secretary. You knew you could always get what you wanted because your hosts were too polite or too uncertain to contradict you, yet you risked ruining the whole effect if they thought you had used your inflated royal authority to get your way. After all, a royal visit was their treat, and sharing in its success was part of that.

The trick was to get your hosts to agree to what you were suggesting, by making them think that it was their idea all along. It took a little longer, and it usually called for lots of that courtier's speciality, schmooze. Nevertheless, it made the host feel good, and a happy host was more than half of a happy royal visit.

I had learned these principles mostly on domestic UK visits, and they were remarkably transportable. It seemed that people expecting a royal guest had very similar expectations whether they were in Kathmandu or Cornwall. The most important one was that the visitor should communicate with them at an informal level. Spontaneity was one of Diana's greatest talents, but it worked best when the hosts – or patients, orphans, ballet dancers or whatever – were themselves in a happy, relaxed frame of mind. That took some organising but, as they say, perfect spontaneity requires thorough planning.

Only the language difference was a problem, but here I discovered that there were surprising compensations. On an earlier recce, to Paris, I had been trying to explain how important it was that the hosts – teenagers, in

Opposite: Royal visits were often an opportunity for displays of traditional dance as here in Kathmandu. Nepal, 1993. By now, Diana was a fully fledged independent royal traveller, representing her charities and her country with equal confidence. For this tour, she was accompanied by Lynda Chalker, a senior minister in the British cabinet.

this case – should feel relaxed and happy when talking to the Princess about what they were doing.

'Do they speak English?' I wondered. Not really, was the reply. I knew Diana's schoolgirl French was not going to bridge the gap. 'So please could they be really busy, surrounded by the things they want to show her, and then Diana and the interpreter will come to them for a chat...' This request was translated as an order for *beaucoup d'animation*, and the phrase so neatly described our requirements that it passed into our reconnaissance glossary. *Beaucoup d'animation* describes that state of happy, humming excitement that should greet any royal visit to almost any activity, except, perhaps, an occasion of high religious ceremony. Even then it was usually possible to apply a variation on the theme, with a bit of imagination.

All this was just more proof that visits by royalty in general, and by Diana in particular, were theatrical shows. That cast the private secretary as the producer, and it proved as accurate a label as any, not least because my job was also to keep the star happy. Keeping the audience happy, though, was more than just a matter of ensuring *beaucoup d'animation*.

I was reminded of the limitations of animation as we were planning Diana's visit to a leprosy community on the outskirts of Kathmandu. As always, the dignity of those she met was a matter of instinctive concern to the Princess and the lepers, many of whom had suffered the stigma of the disease all their lives. Many were coping with leprosy in a particularly disfiguring form. Others were recovering from reconstructive surgery.

Even though we'd make sure no cameras intruded, I knew it would be a challenge to make this engagement as rewarding as it deserved to be for the visitor and visited. Unlike their fellow sufferers in Indonesia, whom Diana had visited in one of my first tours, these patients were shy to the point of invisibility. And here they were, about to face a tall, energetic, blonde western Princess. Scaring everybody out of sight wasn't the aim. In short, I could see that this trip might go badly wrong and, to make matters worse, if I had to stay in London I wouldn't be there to take the rap.

Sensing my worry, one of the saintly nursing staff asked me what was wrong. I tried to explain. She nodded and suggested a solution: in Nepal it wasn't unusual for the king to be disinclined, or unable, to make personal contact with everyone at a gathering. Not receiving such contact was a potentially damaging loss of face. To overcome this, a principle known as *darshan* had been established, according to which mere attendance in the royal presence was considered enough to satisfy the need for personal acknowledgement.

So *darshan* joined *animation* in our lexicon. It helped that Diana, through lively eye contact and general charisma, could lighten up a room of people just by walking in. But the principle of deliberately making even those on the periphery of a royal event an equally valued member was one that we made a conscious effort to follow, wherever in the world we were.

Whatever the reason, Diana's visit to the leprosy community – like the rest of her visit to Nepal – was another conspicuous success. Or so she told me down the phone from Nepal. That was because the stork had been very late and I was still in London. Being daddy.

Before I finish, let me add one other term from the recce dictionary. It pre-dated my arrival but was just as useful as *darshan* or *animation*. At every royal event, attention is rightly concentrated on the immediate royal party. This is most obvious if a member of the Royal Family happens to be sitting at a table, at an official banquet, but the principle applies to any occasion, especially if a formal seating plan is required.

A disproportionate effort goes into getting seating plans exactly right. Every nuance of protocol and general one-upmanship has to be taken into account when deciding which VIP sits where at the top table. No such care is needed for the hangers-on. Assorted equerries, secretaries, body-guards and information officers must also have a table at which to eat, organise their paperwork, rest their aching feet and have a good moan and/or gossip. But nobody cares about them or their seating plan. To the untrained eye they are a bunch of layabouts.

Members of the royal party recuperating in this way deserve a name and once, on a tour long, long ago, a caustic Australian official gave them one. Asked who these assorted royal roadies were, he dismissed them contemptuously as 'bloody *bludgers*!' This translates as social security scroungers. The name stuck and now anyone travelling on the royal coat tails – especially if they are stuffing their faces – is known as a *bludger*. And of course private secretaries have to plan for them too. It's a golden rule: all the *darshan* and *animation* in the world doesn't compensate for one table of unhappy *bludgers*.

Above: Diana had a natural aptitude for the diplomatic skills required to win friends, beginning with her official hosts. Arriving at Kathmandu, 1993.

Moscow

I had visited Russia as a schoolboy and seen some of the main tourist attractions of what was then still a communist state. I had subsequently served a dozen years in the Royal Navy – a service whose main mission was to be prepared for (and so deter) war with the Soviets and their allies.

My time with Diana had seen the collapse of the Berlin Wall and the disintegration of the former USSR. In short, it was a country that fascinated me and was at the top of the global news agenda. It was surely high time that the world's most famous woman paid it a visit, I thought. She did, too.

Although many of Diana's overseas tours were at the request of the Foreign Office (termed official visits), others were initiated by charities and organisations which she helped (working visits), and were given a Foreign Office blessing. They formed the majority of our travels. The rest were made up of private visits.

Although keen to foster good relations with post-communist Russia, the Foreign Office wanted to reserve its royal diplomatic gunpowder for a planned visit by the head of state, the Queen. So when the suggestion was made that Diana might accept an invitation from a Russian children's charity of which she had become patron, the Foreign Office was happy to give its approval as a working visit. We acted as a kind of trailer for the main feature which followed.

The patronage was unusual. For one thing, it is rare for a member of the Royal Family to accept patronage of an organisation outside the Commonwealth. For another, it was known at the outset that the chances of Diana getting involved with it at first hand – as she liked to do – would be limited. Nevertheless, the diplomatic advantages were thought sufficient to justify the link, and so it was that the Princess became patron of the Tushinskaya Children's Hospital in Moscow. (The diplomatic angle was no coincidence. The original suggestion for the affiliation had come from Sir Brian Cartledge, until recently British Ambassador in the Russian capital.

Opposite: Moscow, 1994. Diana in Red Square was a glamorous symbol of the change in international relations since the end of the Cold War.

He became an enthusiastic and invaluable advisor on this project.)

Initially there was no prospect of the Princess actually going to see the hospital for herself. Apart from anything else, her critics at home were suspicious that she was developing an unhealthy appetite for easy foreign photo opportunities. They were wrong, but I didn't want to encourage them. Nor did Diana want the Russians to think that she'd only accepted the honour of patronage so that she could let the light of her countenance shine upon their sick children. It was in her nature to want to be of more practical use than that.

So it was that Tushinskaya became the first beneficiary of a new fund-raising initiative. Diana was in regular demand for movie premieres, always as patron of a charity or two that would share the takings from what were famously lucrative occasions. One drawback, however, was that the film distributor inevitably got involved in negotiations with well-meaning, but sometimes time-consuming, committee meetings and associated charity politics.

After discussion with Warner Brothers and the major UK distributor we streamlined the process. For the next premiere – the Harrison Ford blockbuster *The Fugitive* – the distributor was spared all the committee meetings and just paid a sizeable cheque into The Princess of Wales' Charities Trust. Everybody was happy – especially Tushinskaya, which got the lion's share.

That's why Diana got a particularly warm welcome when she finally flew to Moscow to visit the hospital. It was high summer, and she looked at her most cool and casually glamorous as she toured the wards. She was, of course, a veteran of a thousand bedside chats but here again the language barrier was easily overcome with a smile and her trademark hands-on approach.

The hospital's facilities were impressive in scale, if not yet in technology. But what impressed the Princess most was the dedication of the staff. As she well knew, children's hospitals all over the world attract a particularly

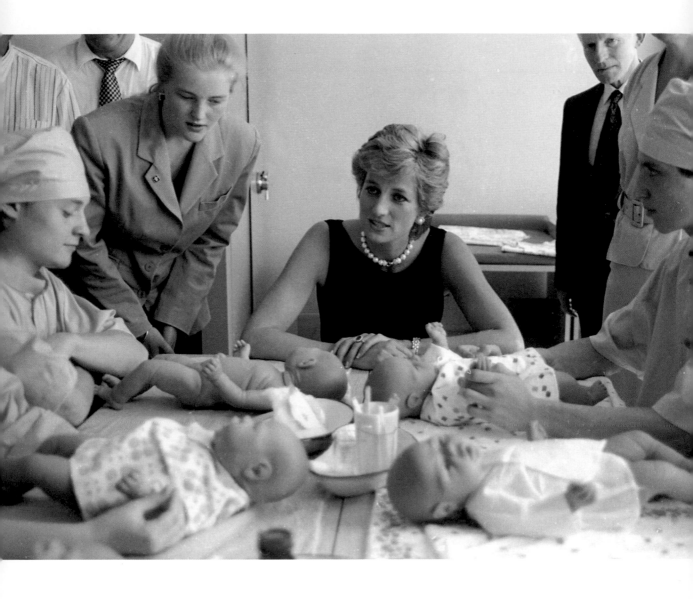

Above: Tushinskaya Children's Hospital. Despite the language barrier, Diana was always fluent in childcare!

'From my place in the royal box behind the Princess, I saw the audience rise to applaud her arrival. It was a powerfully symbolic moment. The Tsarina herself couldn't have looked more regal.'

devoted breed of carer. But, in Tushinskaya, the teamwork between all branches of medical staff and the active involvement of families made a deep impression on her.

Neo-natal care was a particular speciality of the hospital, and Diana lingered among the incubators listening through an interpreter and sharing some of the anxiety of waiting parents. Or so I'm told. Of all the medical sights I encountered in the line of royal duty, the only ones that reduced me to jelly were premature baby units. So as the lady-in-waiting stuck to her post, I found an open doorway and took deep breaths of the flower-scented Russian breeze.

There were more flowers to sniff at the Ambassador's garden party. The British Embassy was still in the darkly forbidding old merchant's house that had been its home through the iciest days of the Cold War. Across the river the famous domes of St Basil's cathedral shone in the afternoon sun, and the red walls of the Kremlin added an impressively austere backdrop. In the embassy garden, however, something like an English country tea party was in full swing with Diana at its centre.

Every visit had a similar celebration. It was a scaled-down version of a Buckingham Palace garden party, a throwback to a gracious age when subjects wore their best outfits, fiddled with a cup of tea and nervously awaited their chance to bow or curtsey. The guests were drawn from the embassy staff, the British Council and other prominent members of the expatriate community, with a sprinkling of local charity reps, commercial contacts and anyone else likely to repay a royal handshake with favours for Britain.

In the early days of her overseas tours, Diana would stand with Charles as an endless line of guests shuffled past, each couple pausing in turn for a 30-second dose of real royal contact. It was an efficient way of making sure that every guest got the handshake they'd been promised, but it was pretty dreary and could be tricky to choreograph smoothly. It only took one over-enthusiastic guest to exceed his ration of royal seconds for the whole line to become snarled. And, sometimes, snarling.

Now, however, the Princess had forged a more spontaneous procedure which required the guests to stand still – preferably in groups of about half a dozen – and she would come to them. With a bit of encouragement, the groups would blend into each other to give the appearance of a comfortably filled space. Add some music and, whenever possible, alcohol and the stage was set for Diana to circulate and chat with all her trademark informality and charm. Everybody agreed this was much better.

In the Moscow sunshine she was at her best. The senior visitors felt that their importance had been duly acknowledged, and the less senior visitors surprised themselves at how much fun it was. So, I suspect, did Diana but she didn't often admit as much.

That evening she went to the Bolshoi. I remembered from my visit as a schoolboy twenty years earlier that the hammer and sickle had incongruously been added to some of the 19th-century plaster decorations. Now the political symbols had disappeared and the imperial splendour had been restored. From my place in the royal box behind the Princess, I saw the audience rise to applaud her arrival. It was a powerfully symbolic moment. The Tsarina herself couldn't have looked more regal.

PART 3 HOSTS WITH THE MOST

'Shall I book these tickets in the name of Ms Pinto?'
Airline agent enquiring about Diana's latest alias

Above: Luciano Pavarotti was a huge admirer of Diana. The feeling was warmly reciprocated, especially after the famous tenor began raising funds for Diana's Charities Trust.

John Latsis (private yacht, *Alexander*)

John Latsis (or 'Captain', as Diana liked to call him) was a billionaire Greek shipping magnate who bought the palatial Bridgewater House, overlooking Green Park, as his London base. He thus became next-door neighbour to the Waleses' office in St James's Palace.

Bridgewater House was given a no-expenses-spared makeover and became a sought-after venue for major charity functions, especially those which included Charles or Diana among the guests. It also became a convenient lunch canteen for world-class conferences, such as the G7 economic summit, held in Lancaster House nearby. This gave important people with pronounced views on taste a chance to make unkind – but very quiet – comments about the Captain's choice of décor.

Like many rich men, especially those for whom London is not their first home, John Latsis correctly judged that the quickest route into society was to spend lavishly on ingratiating himself with influential people. The Waleses were a conveniently close target for this treatment, and they quickly yielded to his advances. For one thing, the sheer scale of his generosity lifted him above the level of the two-a-penny millionaires who were the usual applicants for a place in the royal circle. For another, he was Greek and a Greek monarchist to boot. That put him in favour with exiled King Constantine which, in turn, was sufficient to prove his credentials with the Prince of Wales.

Soon Charles's staff were organising a Mediterranean family cruise on board Latsis's yacht *Alexander* – a huge floating version of Bridgewater House, and every bit as impressive as the Royal Yacht *Britannia*, at least in tonnage.

These were the days – in the late '80s – when Charles and Diana were still being put through the ordeal of pretending to like each other. The cruise would at least give them a chance to keep William and Harry entertained, and also gave the Prince a chance to invite several of his friends. In theory, the yacht would sail a random course around the

Above and next pages: Holidays were a welcome break but after a few days Diana was itching to get back into the London routine of royal work, seeing friends and planning the next trip.

Mediterranean, and thus stay one jump ahead of the paparazzi.

This secret-mission aspect of the preparations didn't make the whole exercise seem any less strange. Nor, in the event, was it a particularly successful ruse. Although many of the English press were tricked off the scent – as Kent Gavin explains in his foreword – *Alexander* was a highly conspicuous visitor to the small ports at which she called. Many paparazzi duly got their shots of William and Harry trying out Latsis' extensive range of jet skis.

I could clearly see that Diana was not much taken by any of it, not least because there was a conspicuous absence of *her* friends. Mercifully, I was not required on the voyage but stories about it – and one which followed it – painted a joyless picture of Diana moping in her cabin or, on a particularly bad day, in a lifeboat. Meanwhile, Charles was allegedly making radio phone calls to Camilla from his own quarters. As if this wasn't bad enough, Diana didn't like the food, the activities, the décor or her fellow guests.

Much of this, including Charles phoning Camilla – she accidentally over-heard the call – she told me when she got home to England. Not surprisingly, she made other arrangements for her holidays with the boys as soon as she and the Prince separated.

But perhaps surprisingly, she remained on good terms with Captain John. She regularly attended events at Bridgewater House, most famously on the very evening that her earth shaking *Panorama* interview was broadcast. And occasionally he would call on her at Kensington Palace, emerging from his limousine in a blue yachting cap which he would doff respectfully to her. He was much more than twice her age, yet flirted with an undiminished gleam in his eye, helped no doubt by his Mediterranean genes and bottomless coffers.

She responded warmly to these courtesies while still managing, gently, to decline all his offers of the free use of his billionaire's toys. Misguidedly, he even offered me the use of a yacht – 'not a big one, Commander, but not

'Accustomed to the almost constant adrenaline rush of her high-wire act in the royal circus, lying in the sun or relaxing with a book did not come naturally to her.'

small either'. It was hard to get the words out but, feeling Diana's eyes drilling into me, I declined. From the Latsis experience, I concluded that Diana had a healthy suspicion of people who might try to put her under an obligation. Though she undoubtedly had a taste for luxury, she knew that Greeks bearing gifts would eventually present a hefty bill.

Her resolve was further strengthened as she watched from the sidelines as the Duke and Duchess of York acquired unenviable reputations as consumers of freebies. Not that she could honestly claim to be an entirely freebie-free zone – there were too many offers of Lear jets to escape them all. But to her credit they were consumed in moderation, discreetly and often in conjunction with her work. After all, as a semi-independent daughter-in-law, it wouldn't have been tactful to make excessive use of the Queen's Flight.

It was doubly poignant, therefore, that after Diana next accepted a free trip on a rich man's Mediterranean yacht, the consequences were to prove infinitely worse than anyone might have feared.

Richard Branson (Virgin Islands)

The Princess of Wales and Richard Branson were two of the most prominent Britons of their generation. Getting them together in one spot would produce a double-charge of media-friendly images… wouldn't it?

Surprisingly, it seemed the answer was 'not really.' Both were, and are, past masters at playing the media to their own advantage. Both had achieved extraordinary personal success without getting much visible help in the process. They were self-made popular favourites. Maybe that was why, on the rare occasions that they did occupy the same stage, the result was somehow less than the sum of the two halves.

Perhaps it was in a gesture of considerate support that Branson offered his paradise island Necker – one of the remaining British islands in the Caribbean – to the besieged Princess. Equally predictably, the world's tabloids were soon packed with telephoto shots of Diana in a swimsuit doing a fair impersonation of Ursula Andress in *Dr No* as she emerged from the surf onto Mr B's beach.

There was no doubt that Diana – and the several members of her family who accompanied her – appreciated the generosity of her host. Peace and quiet were not impossible for her to find (though she generally liked to maintain that they were), but on Necker she had a whole island to herself. It was the kind of place that appealed to her well-developed taste for the kind of luxury that befits royalty. And it gave her a wonderful tan with which to return to wintry London. Even so, she was a restless holiday-maker. Accustomed to the almost constant adrenaline rush of her high-wire act in the royal circus, lying in the sun or relaxing with a book did not come naturally to her. Her quicksilver mind was too impulsive to enjoy a really good bout of sloth, and her talents lay more with real people than with characters on a page.

Though she liked to give the impression of being overworked – most memorably in her melodramatic 'withdrawal' from public life in 1993 – my clear observation was that she was happiest when fully occupied, preferably doing something constructive. In other words, she was just like the rest of us.

It was in her nature to be generous in return. So the Bransons came to a special, if rather subdued, family lunch at Kensington Palace. And pretty soon, after a bit of enthusiastic softening-up by me, Virgin Atlantic found itself sharing the honour with British Airways of flying Diana on her long-haul overseas tours. They were brilliant at it, and regularly made my life as royal travel agent a lot more pleasant. They certainly excelled at making their royal passenger feel at home. The trick was to create the impression of a private jet while retaining the desired media angle that she was just another passenger on a scheduled flight. On at least one occasion, this even extended to leaving many seats unsold to allow for the extra fuel necessary to guarantee that she wouldn't be delayed by an en route stop to top-up the jet's tanks.

In another sign of her admiration, the Princess honoured the tycoon by officially christening one of his new Airbus A340 airliners at a special ceremony at Heathrow airport. Richard, naturally, wanted to name the aircraft *Princess Diana*. I stuffily objected, thinking of potential flak for such a glaring piece of commercial endorsement. Of course I was being need-

Opposite: Diana names a Virgin Airlines Airbus A340 with the help of Richard Branson.

lessly fussy. Had I checked with precedent, I would have discovered that the young Princess Elizabeth had named an airliner *Princess Elizabeth of England* in the 1940s. I wonder if she ever flew to Scotland in it – or Wales or Ireland, for that matter. It only went to show that nobody in the royal organisation had a monopoly on correct form – a reassuring thought as we evolved Diana's own unique style.

With good grace Richard changed the plan, and the Airbus was named *Lady in Red* instead (I'm glad to report that Richard's tribute to his royal friend was not so easily rebuffed; Virgin Atlantic currently flies an airliner named *Lady Diana*). He even arranged for Chris de Burgh to play the famous song at the celebrations. Glitz and aviation were masterfully combined to give Diana the happiest day of a troubled period in her life.

Nevertheless, as the Virgin King cheerfully sprayed champagne in all directions, and manhandled his royal guest of honour through the day's programme, I couldn't help thinking that both stars were in danger of taking a bit too much of each other's limelight.

Luciano Pavarotti (Modena)

Diana was never 'Disco Di'. Yes she was well informed about popular music but it was Charles, not her, who notched up the most pop concerts. In fact she was patron of some great cultural institutions, including the English National Ballet, the Welsh National Opera, the Royal Academy of Music and the London City Ballet.

Most days, when I arrived at Kensington Palace after my stressful drive from the office in St James's Palace, my road rage was calmed by the sound of a soothing overture on Diana's hi-fi. And her piano playing – more expressive than technically expert – testified to her enjoyment of classical music. So when it was suggested that Luciano Pavarotti might be recruited to her fund-raising banner, the Princess, an educated fan, said yes.

The buccaneering impresario Rod Gunner – who had hit the jackpot for

the Princess with his Concerts of Hope starring the boy band Take That! –
was soon making final arrangements. And where better than in Cardiff,
capital of her Principality and home to the most discerning male voice
experts in the world.

The concert in the Cardiff Indoor Arena was a towering success, not just
for Pavarotti – though he can have had few more appreciative audiences
– but also for the Princess. The concert marked a major milestone in her
growth as a fund-raiser in her own right, and for causes that she had
chosen. Given the view that much of modern royalty is a branch of the
charity industry, this was an achievement of real significance.

Diana was usually conscientious about repaying such support. Besides
her desire to thank a friend there was a shrewd ambition to broaden her
power-base among influential figures. Her friendship with Pavarotti was a
valuable commodity to be invested productively.

Pavarotti had his own good causes to support. One of these was the
new charity, War Child, a joint response by famous musicians to the
suffering of children in the Balkans in the early 1990s. Diana was glad to
reciprocate Pavarotti's support, and it took only his offer of a Lear jet to find
her jetting into Modena for his annual music festival.

He greeted her (and, alarmingly, me) with his habitual bear hug before

'As I watched Diana exercising her own celebrity, I saw how she had now evolved into a self-confident, international figure in her own right. She didn't have to dance to anybody else's tune any more.'

leading the way to a lavish back-stage encampment. And it *was* a camp – each performer had an individual tent, like a medieval jouster. They were linked by canvas walkways to a central marquee where our host's personal chef dispensed pasta in what quickly became a sort of exclusive piazza, populated by promenading superstars.

Diana had her own tent, a modest version of Pavarotti's next door. Her other neighbours were members of U2 who invited her into what was already a homely stopping point for other performers in search of a beer and a chat. Soon she was mixing happily with the Cranberries, Meatloaf, Bono, Simon LeBon and others. As I watched Diana exercising her own celebrity, I saw how she had now evolved into a self-confident, international figure in her own right. She didn't have to dance to anybody else's tune any more.

David Tang (Hong Kong and Venice, 1995)

'You can rely on David Tang 110%,' said Chris Patten, the last Governor of Hong Kong. We were sitting in his office in Government House, that quaint relic of imperial architecture now overshadowed by the great sky-scrapers that had grown up around it. His words didn't come as a surprise. David Tang's name had produced the same reaction in practically

everybody else I had asked. From my initial contacts with him, I was beginning to share their high opinion.

Already a famous figure in Hong Kong – where his trademark retro Chinese fashion store was an essential landmark for the serious shopper – the anglicised entrepreneur was now a rising star in the London social sky. Like many before him, he recognised that a judicious bit of royal contact could only accelerate his ascent into the social stratosphere. Unlike many of them, however, he made nothing but friends along the way. That was partly because he went about the process with his usual efficiency and flair. But mostly it was because he was such a nice chap.

Thus it was that, as Prince Charles boarded the Royal Yacht *Britannia* to mark the end of British rule in Hong Kong, bidding him farewell was not only the departing Governor, Chris Patten, but the unmistakable figure of David.

After my meeting with Chris Patten, I did my recce (with David's help) for a visit the Princess was due to make in 1995. I'd been to Hong Kong before with the Prince and Princess, and before that as a junior officer in the navy. I loved the place, and now there was no better or more generous host with whom to see it than David.

He had a reputation as a major benefactor of local charities – everything from cancer hospitals to the sea cadets – and now he was proposing to add a royal diamond to his glittering philanthropic record. The Princess was his target and he hit the bull's eye – he would underwrite and help co-ordinate a short fund-raising tour of Hong Kong, culminating in a dinner at his ultra-cool China Club.

It would be the social event of the Hong Kong year. It would benefit some highly deserving charities, including the Princess's own patronage, the Leprosy Mission, which was doing unsung work in mainland China. Best of all, it would help Diana develop a new style of visit which could become a pattern for future tours.

The main characteristics of this new style were clear. It was to be highly

efficient in raising large sums for good causes through a small investment in royal time; it wouldn't be a drain on public funds; and it was secure in media terms, having the support of a respected local figure (David) and the Queen's representative (Governor Patten). Finally, it would provide some very attractive photos for the glossies back home, and would be a lot of fun.

Professionally, I wasn't interested in fun. Instead, it was part of my job to vet the large numbers of wealthy men who tried to ingratiate themselves with the Princess. On the face of it, David Tang fell into this category. But he quickly proved to be the best example of a rarer type: those who bring more to the equation – in terms of donations and good company – than they take out in royal kudos.

I had to be alert to the fact that the charity concerts, gala dinners and celebrity auctions in big cities were hunting grounds for predatory philanthropists in search of royal trophies. They were generally men who had

Above: David Tang was the inspiration behind two of Diana's most successful trips.

acquired every material possession they could want, and now wanted the one thing that wasn't for sale: the company of royalty. And the shiniest model in the showroom was HRH The Princess of Wales.

For her part, Diana knew the game in all its nuances. She knew that, in the guise of helping out a favourite royal cause, royal company certainly could be bought. She knew that at least part of the reason why so many charities had her name on their letterhead was that she was expected to give these rich royal groupies a good shakedown. She knew that heartrending photocalls with sick children was one part of her role and, for her, the most rewarding part. But she also knew that she was just as much use to her favourite causes dressed up in a Versace frock bestowing handshakes and smiles to would-be benefactors. For better or worse, it's how a lot of modern fund-raising works.

And though she invariably performed above and beyond the call of duty for her charities – dancing with dubious tycoons, charmingly parrying their attempts at flirtation and silently sympathising with their wives – the act took its toll. In the car back to Kensington Palace, her scent mixing with the lingering cigar smoke, she would laugh with relief but also with cool insight: 'Honestly, Patrick, they'd put their money in the dustbin if I told them to!'

David Tang was a cut above these scavengers of royal favour. He didn't dance with her, didn't flirt with her – except in the best way, by making her laugh – and, in those days, he didn't have a wife who deserved her sympathy. True, he was always suffused with cigar smoke but, in every important respect, he was the model benefactor whose royal prey was always happy to come back for more.

Diana's crowded but spectacularly successful Hong Kong tour of 1995 was one of the happiest I ever experienced. I think Diana felt the same. As well as the cheerful high tempo of her charity and fund-raising engagements, David and I had also made time for a return visit to the drug rehabilitation island at Shek Kwu Chau. The tranquillity of the place once again allowed her a few moments of calm.

It was no surprise that David's subsequent appearance at Diana's side – at the Venice *Biennale* exhibition – was an equally entertaining experience. Never more so than when he was temporarily stranded on a jetty as the Princess's boat sped off across the lagoon (it's a rule of royal transport: you had to be quick if you didn't want to get left behind). He could barely be seen through clouds of spray and exhaust smoke, a rapidly disappearing figure, resplendent in a canary yellow silk tunic. I could just hear his plaintive call above the roar of the engines: 'Where the f*** are we going next?!'

This was one of my last trips with Diana. Our working relationship was already showing signs of terminal strain as she tried, unsuccessfully in my view, to plot a straight course among the distractions of her uncertain solo status. With the jagged reef of the *Panorama* interview broadcast fast approaching, it could certainly be said that we were all at sea. As a commentary on our situation, I thought David's words were just about perfect.

A private visit – the bodyguard's story, by Ken Wharfe

After Diana's first solo visit to Paris in 1992, she was determined to return but this time incognito. 'I just want to go shopping with a couple of girl-friends,' she said. 'I want to be normal.' Nice idea, I thought. But the practicalities of sneaking the most famous woman in the world into the French capital without the papparazi noticing were formidable. I had to do my best.

The girlfriends were Hyatt Palumbo (wife of the property tycoon Lord [Peter] Palumbo) and Lucia Fleccha de Lima (wife of the Brazilian Ambassador to London, and arguably the best friend Diana ever had). Thanks to Peter Palumbo a private jet was provided to take the shopping party and me to Paris. I had arranged for anonymous cars to meet us at the low-profile airfield outside the city that I had selected for our arrival. The glamorous shoppers climbed in like schoolgirls on an outing, and nobody knew we were there. It all worked perfectly.

We headed straight for the Chanel boutique where they enjoyed a private fashion show. Then we toured a few more exclusive emporiums – including Hermes where Diana bought me a tie – before dossing down for the night at the Palumbos' award-winning residence near the Bois de Boulogne. Next day our luck continued to hold. Diana and her friends spent a few more thousand pounds in Paris couturiers (it didn't take long), and then decided to break for lunch in the exclusive Marius et Jeanette restaurant. Still we were undetected. But our luck was about to run out.

As the Princess and her friends went to their table, they didn't know that they had walked into the viewfinder of one of France's most formidable photographers. Jean-Paul Dousset worked with the notorious don of the paparazzi, Daniel Angelli. He had broken a score of photo-journal scandals, most recently the Duchess of York's affair with Johnny Bryant. Now I spotted him lurking outside the restaurant and his Nikon motordrive was in action.

Luckily, Diana didn't see him as they started lunch, oblivious to the fact that their secret holiday was about to become headline news. I wondered how Dousset had learned of our plans. Then it hit me. Sitting across the room was the unmistakable figure of Gerard Depardieu. Dousset had been staking him out, and presumably couldn't believe his scoop as Diana wandered in. If I acted immediately, there was a chance that Diana's holiday could be saved…

Depardieu provided a useful distraction. Quickly recognising the Princess, he crossed the room to her table and began to exercise his renowned Gallic charm on her. She was a willing recipient. They began a lively, flirtatious conversation. Briefly excusing myself, I slipped back outside and quietly confronted the photographer. He was taken aback but perfectly polite. We had a brief and productive discussion and eventually struck a deal: so long as he remained discreetly in the background so that Diana didn't notice him, I wouldn't interfere with his work. He would also withhold the pictures until we had left France so that she wouldn't be mobbed, and I wouldn't face an increased security risk.

It worked. For the rest of the day Dousset trailed us at a tactful distance, and didn't release his impressive, lucrative haul of photos until we had left the country. Diana enjoyed her holiday undisturbed, and I had nipped in the bud a situation that might have turned into a major publicity and security incident.

The episode was a good example of one of the pitfalls of guarding the world's most recognisable woman. It was just one of many occasions when I, and Diana's other bodyguards, had to combine press management with our primary security duties. Often, as this incident shows, the two went hand in hand. But the subtle problems of trying to keep everybody happy were seldom properly understood, I felt, by my Scotland Yard bosses.

I could see why. Their procedures were designed for the reliably predictable behaviour of the older and lower profile members of the Royal Family. But Diana attracted a degree of attention that other bodyguards seldom had to deal with. She also led an increasingly complicated private lifestyle in which even well-meaning minders were often unwelcome. So in this, as in so much else, we had to make up new procedures especially for her on the spur of the moment.

Diana's protection officers had to compromise and improvise in ways that never appeared on a training syllabus. That sometimes made us – and I suppose, as the senior officer, me in particular – objects of suspicion among the conservative ranks of higher management. Still, as the tired but happy shoppers flew back from Paris, I thought that was a price worth paying.

PART 4 PRINCESS ALONE

'The power of her appeal was
vulnerable fallibility.'

Simon Schama

Above: A pensive Diana waits to make her acceptance speech at the 1995 Humanitarian of the Year Awards. Despite sustained work to improve her public speaking technique, she never completely overcame her nerves.

Tokyo

The Tokyo tour almost didn't happen. In fact by 1995, organising a tour for Diana had become a bit like organising a picnic in a minefield. Old familiar pathways through the Palace/Whitehall undergrowth had become all but impassable. By blazing a new trail as an independent royal traveller, Diana risked detonating explosions of opposition from a growing list of critics. To many of them, she was an unpredictable threat to the royal establishment and hence someone to be intimidated or belittled into obscurity.

Her status as a separated but not yet divorced Princess of Wales was unprecedented. Nobody knew how to interpret the Queen's wish that Diana no longer represent her abroad – a happy outcome so far as I was concerned. It meant I was able to assume that the only way to find the limits of Diana's freedom was for her to go on making working visits abroad until someone said stop. And provided Diana was seen to make a good job of representing, if not the Queen, then at least her country, while abroad, then who would have the courage to express their public opposition?

The answer, of course, was nobody. Instead, Diana's detractors, most of whom presumed the tacit approval of her husband's camp, were reduced to briefing against her in the press – predictably she briefed right back – or patronisingly pretended she was a lightweight who should be ignored.

The Japanese, and other foreigners, were happily ignorant of these attempts to hobble the Princess. Even if they had fully comprehended the opposition Diana faced at home, her overseas hosts would have been rightly contemptuous of such petty squandering of such an obvious national asset. Instead, irrespective of whether she was representing the Queen, presidents and prime ministers lined up to meet and be photographed with her.

To Diana's admirers around the world her appeal was above national

Opposite: This was one of Diana's favourite dresses so she wore it on several occasions including a Washington gala in 1991 and (as here) at a reception in Tokyo in 1990.

identity. And Foreign Secretaries seemed quicker than some courtiers to appreciate what Diana could do. Lord (Douglas) Hurd was in charge of British foreign policy for most of my time with the Princess and, after her death, wrote in the *Daily Telegraph*:

> *She had discovered in herself the power of compassion – the ability to enter into the anxieties and sufferings of others. She wanted to use this power abroad as well as at home… that was what the Princess meant when she spoke of being an ambassador. As far as I am concerned, her visits did nothing but good…*

There was an unwelcome prelude to Diana's Tokyo tour. The publication of photos (taken using a concealed camera) revealed her exercising in a gym. They showed an impressively fit Diana in fresh make-up and a fashionably skimpy leotard. She was livid. Through her solicitor, I organised a legal counter-attack which was reaching its climax as we flew east. And although I felt some sympathy for her outrage, I was frustrated that such an essentially petty incident should be hogging the media limelight.

It wasn't just petty, it was also very avoidable. I knew that Diana was quite prepared to recruit sympathetic media attention when it suited her. I also knew that her fondness for public gyms was a conscious policy that regularly produced flattering images and comments about her increasingly well-honed physique. If the policy had backfired this time – and deep down I found her protestations unconvincing – then she couldn't honestly claim to be a completely innocent victim. But the image of victim was too tempting for her to resist.

The trouble was, the only real victim was her credibility as a serious international figure. Here was the Princess embarking on another overseas mission, flying the flag for Britain and several charities before an important world audience. It was a vital reaffirmation of her value as an independent royal operator in defiance of her critics. Yet most public attention was

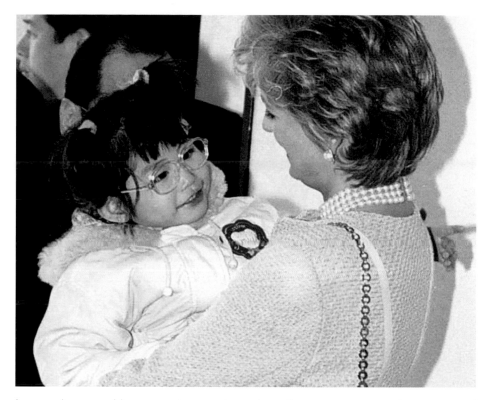

being distracted by speculation about the effectiveness – or otherwise – of her exercise regime in an obscure suburban fitness centre.

I swallowed my anger. While in Tokyo, in the middle of the night, I was woken to be told that Diana had won an apology from the tabloid that had published the photographs. Using the code we had invented, I pushed a piece of paper under her bedroom door: 'The man from Del Monte – he say Yes!' She knew what I meant. And the tour was a huge success, including a very regal cup of tea with the Emperor and his family at the Imperial Palace.

As I watched Diana curtsey her farewell to the Emperor I told myself not to be so uncharitable. So what if she had partly brought the sneaky photo drama on herself? She still did the best curtsey in the business. And she looked pretty good in a leotard too.

'It marked the end of an era – six years in which Diana's overseas tours had been the high-profile component of her bid for independence within the royal system.'

Buenos Aires

An extraordinary tour, and a sad one.

It was extraordinary, coming hard on the heels of Diana's dramatic – and, I thought, disastrous – *Panorama* interview which effectively marked the final extinction of her chances of working with, if not inside, the Royal Family. Sad because, apart from a few days in New York the following month, this was the last time I accompanied the Princess overseas. It was also the last time she travelled abroad as representative of her country.

On both counts, it marked the end of an era – six years in which Diana's overseas tours had been the high-profile component of her bid for independence within the royal system. It had supplied her supporters with tangible evidence of her qualities as an ambassador for good causes and for British diplomacy. At the same time, it had supplied her critics with nothing. After Argentina, all that would change. She would essentially be on her own and, ultimately, vulnerable to the flawed protection of people who were unable to keep her, or her reputation, safe.

The prospect of hopping onto a jumbo jet to fly south seemed irresistible. The atmosphere in wintry Britain was turbulent, to say the least, as the after-effects of Diana's *Panorama* bombshell hung over our heads like an angry black cloud. And I was still wrestling with the implications of her decision

Top left: The Argentinians gave Diana an enthusiastic welcome. Top right: President Menem may not have been as tall as Diana... but they nevertheless plainly enjoyed each other's company. The President's daughter joined the official lunch and introduced her puppy to the Princess. Bottom: Her hosts were keen to show Diana a friendly whale in the sea off Patagonia. Luckily the whale appeared right on cue!

to keep the interview secret from me until it was too late for me to stop it. In eight years together, Diana and I had forged a strong working relationship. But now it was clearly coming to an end. For many months, my self-preservation instincts had been telling me I should resign and, after *Panorama*, it was only a matter of time. For now though, we both needed to escape the freezing disapproval blowing from the outraged royal establishment and I could temporarily forget my resignation dilemma in the familiar bustle of an overseas tour.

This tour was anything but easy. Memories of the Falklands War were still painfully fresh. Diplomatic contacts with Argentina were still fragile. And, at home, the Princess's enemies would seize on any slip-up as proof of her unworthiness as a national representative. The stakes were high.

From Buckingham Palace I detected polite watchfulness; from Charles's office at St James's Palace I detected even less enthusiasm. The prospect of Diana adding more laurels to her collection, in the wake of her prime-time attack on the Prince, must have been a galling prospect for his camp.

As a precaution, therefore, I had taken more care than usual to make sure that the government was wholeheartedly behind the trip. In doing so I had the reassuring knowledge that Diana's overseas record was unblemished – in fact she was a consistently excellent emissary. It would have been hard to imagine an envoy better calculated to inspire warm sentiments from her Latin hosts. And so it proved.

With the Foreign Secretary's letter of approval in my coat pocket, I waited at the foot of the stairs in Kensington Palace. This was the tensest moment: we were ready to go. Still, even after all these years, a little voice niggled in my head. Were we *really* ready?

The advance party of protection officer and press secretary were already in Buenos Aires. Their initial despatches had been reassuring: the Embassy was on top of everything and, crucially, our hosts were not suggesting any helpful 'improvements' to the agreed programme. The baggage master was already on his way to Heathrow with the special lorry British Airways helpfully sent for the occasion.

Making sure we had all the necessities was a big worry. We carried everything from 12 changes of clothes for the Princess to computer printer cartridges, from official gifts to special mourning stationery in case of a royal death while away (that's why I always took a black tie), and from emergency blood supplies for the Princess (she belonged to a rare blood group) to her favourite wholemeal bread for breakfast. Too late to worry now, I told myself, and focused on my check-list.

In my briefcase I had the essential tools of my trade – the Princess's diary and my notebook, spare stationery, a couple of important programme files (the rest were on the lorry), the pocket and detailed version of the programme, and a copy of the administrative instructions.

These last few items were minor works of art. The detailed version of the programme contained, as the name implies, a comprehensive list of timings for every one of the Princess's engagements. There were also the names, titles and brief job descriptions of every person she was likely to meet in each place. There was an explanatory diagram of the route she was to take through every building she visited showing where to expect line-ups of dignitaries, positions of crowds and safety barriers, the composition of vehicle convoys and locations of press pens.

There were seating plans for banquets and dinners, and even seating plans for where people should sit *after* dinner. There were seating plans for cars and aeroplanes. And – a nice touch – lists of who was to get into which lift in certain buildings. The details went on and on. It was a format that I had embellished over the years so that each little volume – with covers in the colour of the national flag of the country we were visiting – had become a labour of love, with extra emphasis on the labour.

The pocket version was small enough to slip into the royal handbag. The administrative instructions went into even more exhaustive detail. You can imagine why my greatest dread was a last-minute decision by our hosts to change as much as a single comma in my master plan. It sometimes happened. In Indonesia one of the first things we had to do on arrival was bin one hundred copies of these beautiful documents and start again almost from scratch. That cost a lot of sleep.

I also carried drafts of the speeches the Princess was due to make in case she wanted to look at them on the flight, and some diverting routine correspondence that we hadn't got around to finishing. There were moments when humdrum paperwork could bring a stabilising whiff of normality to the most exotic foreign surroundings. And it always paid to have some impressive state papers to hand if Diana wanted to look busy, and avoid making small talk with a boring host.

Finally, I had to take little trinkets (for example, cufflinks for boys and purses or notepads for girls, all emblazoned with her royal cipher, an elaborate 'D' with a coronet on top) that Diana liked to have immediately available to express appreciation for any act of service that sparked her gratitude. And since she was usually an appreciative visitor, we tended to give out quite a lot.

At the end of the tour she would hold a formal prize-giving ceremony at which she would personally thank key members of the embassy staff and the host government for their contribution. That required considerable quantities of signed photographs and other goodies. They were already on their way to Heathrow with the other heavy baggage. Or so I hoped.

Waiting at the front door, I knew, was an estate car parked behind the Princess's Jaguar. Into this second vehicle the dresser was putting the last few pieces of the Princess's cabin baggage. The ritual of the royal cabin baggage was one I'd been witnessing for more than six years, and it still impressed me. At our destination, Diana had to emerge from the aeroplane looking immaculate. Over the years, much to the relief of the dresser, the Princess had gradually – and considerately – pared down the amount of onboard kit she required to achieve what was obviously still a near-perfect result.

So, everything was as ready as it could be… but where was the star of the show? Diana was normally very time conscious. 'Punctuality is the courtesy of kings,' she quoted to me more than once, usually when I, as timekeeper, had caused some glitch in the smooth running of her programme.

Suddenly I heard her footsteps and looked up to see her cantering down the broad green-carpeted staircase of Kensington Palace. She had an air of half-suppressed excitement, as she always did when setting off on an important trip. Her expression was friendly and business-like. It was the Princess at her best. She was reacting with her usual tough defiance to the pressures of the last few days. She was going to confound her detractors with a copybook display of how to be the perfect professional royal celebrity.

Seeing her mood, my optimism returned. We had a show to get on the road. I put aside thoughts of resignation.

But within weeks the Queen would order Charles and Diana to finalise their divorce. Like many aggrieved wives, Diana needed tactical freedom to fight her legal corner effectively, but where would that leave my primary loyalty to the Crown? For the first time in all my years with her, I knew without doubt that supporting the Princess would mean opposing the Queen. The fact that the Family Division of the High Court of Justice would dispense its ruling in the name of her mother-in-law didn't make me feel much better.

These thoughts compounded my dismay at the *Panorama* interview, and brought to a head my growing disagreements with Diana about her future course. Our work became tainted by mistrust. By the time I eventually resigned two months later, I'm sad to say that leaving her felt more like an escape.

But even as I packed up my briefcase for the last time, I knew that every mile with Diana had been not just an adventure, it had been a privilege.

Paris

Beauty attracts beauty. Paris and Diana made a natural couple, now forever linked in history. It was tragically apt that the scene of so many high-points of her life should also have been the scene of her death.

I wasn't with her on her final visit to the city in 1997. Nor, more to the point, were any of her devoted veteran protection officers. The pursuit of a controversial love affair was no place for a private secretary, even if I hadn't long since resigned. And Diana had already unwisely, in my view, placed her safety in the hands of well-meaning but relatively inex-perienced new guardians. Two days after her death I met one of the protection officers whom she had chosen not to use on that visit. I was shocked to see this strong man in tears. 'We wouldn't have let this happen to her, Patrick!' He may have been right.

Most of Diana's days in Paris were more than happy. They were triumphant. Very early in my time at St James's there had been a joint visit with Charles, for which my opposite number, the Prince's equerry, was on duty so I stayed back at base in St James's Palace. Despite the terminal tensions within the marriage, that tour had been a huge success, at least diplomatically and pictorially. But Diana had noted the Parisians' particular fondness for her – and it went deeper than traditional French admiration for a beautiful woman who had a model's eye and figure for drop-dead fashion. It was also a recognition that she was at least potentially a major operator in her own right, not just the appendage of her more conventional husband.

This appealed to a large section of the French public, especially when Diana returned for subsequent visits not just as a solo act but as a popular rebel. French commentators cared little for the rights and wrongs of the Morton book, the Hewitt affair or the Squidgygate tapes. All they saw was that Diana was throwing off the shackles of a suffocating royal marriage. In the home of the French Revolution, the Bastille and the guillotine, that was

Above: Aside from his French charm and forthright style (his nickname is 'Le Bulldozer') President Chirac had one extra qualification that made him particularly attractive to Diana – he was taller than her. Bottom left: One of the last shots taken of Diana, as she relaxes at St Tropez in 1997. Bottom right: Diana left an enigmatic message when she told photographers that she had a surprise in store.

just the sort of image that was guaranteed to win passionate Gallic hearts. If the image was popular, so was the reality. Diana went to Paris to work, not pose, although if the French decided she was an icon of style then that was okay by her.

Diana normally flew the flag for British *couture* when travelling abroad, but on visits to France she made a special effort to honour French design houses by wearing some of their most striking creations. This was a shrewd move, and typical of her awareness that what she wore could be a powerful channel of communication.

Before any tour I had to advise her on popular local colours, perceptions of modesty, hazards (such as awkward steps or revealing camera angles) and other potential 'wardrobe malfunctions' as the Americans say. Not that Diana needed much guidance beyond these snippets of local knowledge. She knew what would appeal to fashion-watchers and never disappointed them.

Nor did she disappoint the many humanitarian and cultural causes she championed in France. Every visit had a carefully structured programme of public duties at its core. The fashion and other glamorous frills were just the accessories.

Which is perhaps why during her years of greatest glamour and influence, there was never an inkling of the disaster to come. Except perhaps one. Driving from the airport to the British Embassy I sat with the Ambassador in his car. In front of us, Diana and the lady-in-waiting travelled in the royal limousine. On either side the convoy was flanked by French motorcycle police. In other countries, this display of leather-clad horsepower and machismo was often the host police force's contribution to the drama – they were looking cool, not looking for threats.

Not in Paris. Here the paparazzi were the apaches of the media. Their mustangs were Kawasaki bikes and their tomahawks were Nikon cameras, and they wheeled and swooped on the royal convoy as if it were a wild-west wagon train. I had never seen anything like it. Waves of photographers – some with TV cameramen riding pillion – raced alongside us, knee to knee with our gesticulating escort. Other cops, some dressed as bikers, drove straight at the raiders, riding them off in a dozen high-speed duels.

When we arrived at the sanctuary of the Embassy, Diana emerged from her car unshaken. In fact her eyes had an extra sparkle. There could hardly have been a more exciting demonstration of her star status. And this seemed to be the general reaction. Outriding an ambush by the Paris motorcycle paparazzi was regarded as a kind of sport.

Perhaps the Princess's acute sense of self-preservation gradually lost its edge during her years cocooned in layers of security. As with much else that could do her harm, Diana seemed to regard the rare but sharp reality of fear as a sensation to be explored, rather than a warning to be heeded. In fact, I sometimes thought she felt herself immune to danger, especially when in a car.

I've since wondered if that false sense of invulnerability infected others the night she died. We now know that neither she nor Dodi Fayed felt the need to wear a seatbelt in the back of the speeding Mercedes. But then again, as I had seen on many occasions, she hardly ever did.

TRAVELS OF A ROYAL PRESS SECRETARY
BY DICKIE ARBITER

Above: Dickie on location in Nigeria, discussing photocall tactics with a group of Fleet Street's finest.

When I began working with the Prince and Princess of Wales, in 1988, their marriage was already falling apart, so a lot of my time was spent trying to avoid this becoming a media headline, and papering over the cracks.

Probably the toughest part of my job was trying to maintain an honest and professional reputation with journalists. They could read the deteriorating marriage signs alright, but the Prince and Princess chose to remain silent on the state of their marriage, and it wasn't for me to bring it to a head. If, by ducking and weaving, journalists thought I was being dishonest then so be it, but at the time it was the right course of action. Despite the domestic troubles, though, Charles and Diana were still a good double act, and one of my roles was to present them in the best possible light at home and overseas.

On a visit to the Gulf, in 1989, I had negotiated some good press positions – equal numbers for the local home press and us, the visitors – promising good pictures and coverage. But someone had forgotten to tell me that in the Gulf V VIPs have their own TV crews and photographers who can go anywhere at any time. So when the V VIP swept in closely followed by his TV crew and photographers, the corralled visiting press contingent were left with shots of a scrum of local journalists. Mayhem followed and our press didn't get pictures worth publishing. I'm pleased to say an incident like that only happened once. But you could always bet there'd be some kind of blip affecting the media or one of the Palace team. The equerry for the 1989 Indonesia trip was Lieutenant Commander Patrick Jephson, RN, and he, with a royal protection officer and me, arrived in the Indonesian capital three days ahead of the Prince and Princess. The QANTAS flight out was uneventful but long. It seemed the only person in seventh heaven at 40,000ft was the equerry. If he wasn't up in the cockpit, he'd be in his seat with a glass of claret in one hand and a flying manual in the other.

When we eventually hit the deck running in Jakarta, Patrick, to his dismay, discovered his ceremonial sword – a family heirloom – had not been unloaded from our aeroplane and was now 3,500 miles away in Sydney. A few hasty phone calls to London and the might of St James's Palace got the sword on the first available aircraft and we all heaved a sigh of relief. An equerry without his sword is a bit like the monarch without his crown.

Above: Diana and Harry share a quiet moment during a major state ceremony – the VJ Day celebrations. August 1995.

The Princess of Wales' first major solo visit abroad – a visit she described as being 'very grown up' – was to New York, in 1989. A good meaty programme had been planned that included a mix of community and charity events, flying the flag for UK plc and the arts, and a big press contingent from both the Americans and the British.

One of the engagements was to the AIDS paediatric unit at Harlem Hospital. The US State Department, responsible for the Princess's security, was concerned about the political leanings of the unit's head, whom they described as being of Irish descent with strong republican sympathies. Given its way, the State Department would have cancelled that part of the visit, but this would have created an even bigger story than it already was. Although the Princess could charm even the most rabid republican, we did brief her on what to expect.

In the end all concern was unfounded. The doctor was bowled over by the Princess and, at a press conference afterwards, he said 'the Princess had done more in her short visit than all the 'American royalty' put together had ever done'.

Everywhere the Prince and Princess travelled, they attracted huge crowds of people and Hungary, in 1990, was no exception. It had just shaken off decades of communist rule and eagerly awaited the first-ever official royal visit. We knew there'd be a large turn out for a Wales Tour (as we called them), so we recommended crowd barriers during the walkabouts in Budapest.

The Hungarians told us in no uncertain terms that 'barriers keep people in, and Hungary is now a democracy, so there would be no barriers'. But despite warnings that things would get out of hand, the first walkabout went ahead sans barriers. Within minutes of arriving in Budapest's famous covered food market, the Prince and Princess were swamped and struggled through the melee of people wanting to shake their hands. Where were the media during this scrum? Always one step ahead of the game, they'd got into a high position and produced some of the best shots of the

tour. Ironically, by the time they arrived for their second walkabout beside the River Danube, the barriers were up. We never imposed our will on any host country, but gently persuaded them that experience over the years had taught us it's better to be safe than sorry.

Getting the media around a country always featured high on my agenda, and never more so than on the 1990 Nigeria and Cameroon tour. There was a lot of travelling over long distances, and the only way to get the 130-strong British media around was to charter an aircraft. At first sight of the local Nigerian Boeing 737 my heart sank. But I was told that because it was regularly serviced at Manchester airport, it was reliable. My doubts subsided as we took off for the round trip to Port Harcourt, the oil capital in the west of Nigeria. But my confidence was short lived.

After 24 hours in Maiduguri, in the north-east of the country, we'd loaded the media contingent and were ready for the off. We sat on the apron with the aircraft's doors closed for nearly half an hour when the doors were thrown open again, and the captain left the aircraft.

I feared we were stuck with a broken plane not going anywhere. But it was a hitch of a different kind. The airport manager had apparently developed a rather lucrative sideline. He claimed the landing fees hadn't been

Above: Without proper preparation there was always the risk that press would get too close. Diana didn't mind this time…

paid and, to prevent the aircraft from leaving, he parked the airport's fire tender in front of the nose wheel. A lot of shouting and arm waving ensued but, eventually, the tender was moved and we left. The press pack oblivious to the drama, were just pleased to have some quiet time.

Without doubt the worst year on a Wales Tour was in 1992, with India at the beginning and South Korea at the end. In February, after a polo match in Jaipur at which the Princess presented trophies and medals, we had the kiss that wasn't. Collecting his medal at the end of the match, the Prince leaned forward to give Diana a peck on the cheek, she turned away and his lips landed firmly on her ear. The press had their story with pictures saying more than any words could reveal.

Above: It was sometimes a tall order to present the Royal Family as a happy, cohesive organisation.

The Princess's visit to the Taj Mahal was another case in point. It was not helped when twelve years earlier the Prince, on a similar visit, had said, 'one day I would like to bring my wife here'. Well, she was and he wasn't. I set up that photo opportunity but, in my defence, it was a picture that would have happened anyway because every VIP visit to the Taj Mahal is photographed from exactly the same spot.

If the India visit sent out clear smoke signals on the state of the marriage, the Princess's solo visit to Budapest a few months later in May helped build them into storm clouds. The first question I was asked on arriving in the Hungarian capital was whether the Princess had co-operated with the former royal watcher, Andrew Morton, whose book was to be published a few weeks later. I confronted the Princess with the allegations, but she swore to me the allegations were untrue. I didn't believe her, but how do you tell a member of the Royal Family that they're being economical with the truth?

But by November and the visit to South Korea, the writing really was on the wall. As the aircraft doors opened everyone saw the Prince and Princess. I turned to the royal protection officer next to me and said, 'Oh God! We've lost it.' The body language between them was non-existent, and neither made any effort to improve the situation. On the face of it, the tour to South Korea was of two royal people on a solo visit to the same country at the same time. The images were clearly of two people disengaged with each other.

The press pack knew it and sent the most telling pictures back to their picture editors. It didn't help either when a reporter was told by one of the royal party, when quizzed about the state of the royal marriage, that all marriages have their difficulties and this one was no different. Four weeks later the end of the marriage became official.

In five years I'd been to twenty-seven countries and been responsible for thirty of their overseas visits – but now Wales Tours, as we knew them, were over forever.

PART 5 DIANA'S STYLE

by Ollie Picton-Jones
Fashion Director *Daily Mirror*

'Few of us will ever look as beautiful on the outside as she did, but all of us can strive to develop that inner beauty of the heart and soul that she valued and understood was more lasting and important.'
Hillary Clinton

'She didn't have a particular way of dressing. She wasn't that strong of an aesthetic presence. [Jackie] Kennedy had a stronger view on how things should look. What will be remembered is that figure, by that I mean the personage moving about in those simple clothes.'
Anne Hollander, fashion historian

'For us…her contribution is immeasurable and irreplaceable.'
John Wilson, British Fashion Council

In 1983 the Princess of Wales was still finding her feet in the fashion world, struggling slightly to choose clothes that expressed her personality yet reflected acceptable royal style. First and foremost, clothes had to be appropriate to the occasion. Here she is visiting an International Spring Fair at Birmingham's NEC; function had to go hand-in-hand with day-time fashion. Her chunky Laura Ashley-style velvet coat dress with a pie-crust collar and cuffs in contrasting white was typical of the era. It is nicely fitted and shows off her figure, and the two stand-up collars are cleverly cut to complement each other while being emphasised by the raglan sleeve detail at the shoulders.

By 1988 Princess Diana had joined the ranks of Jackie Onassis and Audrey Hepburn as a world-famous fashion icon, revered internationally for her unique sense of style and elegance, whatever the occasion. Here she broke all the rules by stepping out in a sophisticated black trouser suit that had been specially designed for her, emulating a man's tuxedo' dinner suit. She was always the first to set new trends, and here she adapted formal men's wear to an elegant ladies look for the evening, and carried it off with great panache. The fashion press applauded such a brave independent spirit who was introducing a bit of wit into the stuffy royal realms, which was one reason why she became a best-selling *Vogue* cover girl many times over.

Above: Princess Diana relished royal gatherings like this one, the Queen Mother's birthday at Clarence House, in 1990, despite her obvious differences with Charles. Her hot pink floral skirt suit screamed 'look at me', being searingly colourful, curvy with its tie-front detail and above all, very photogenic. She wore it with casual confidence, no hat, bag or gloves, just simple pearl drop earrings and a warm, honey-gold suntan. As always, she stole the show with her 'English rose' look, and her bold and breezy fashion statement. This was a typical example of the stand-alone style; she knew the power lay in the lens, and she worked it at every opportunity.

Above right: Diana is pictured here visiting a Cancer Hospital and Research Centre in Pakistan, in 1996, appropriately dressed in a flowing green and blue printed shalwar kameez that she has personalised with matching high-heeled suede shoes. With her western hairstyle, chunky pearl earrings, tortoiseshell sunglasses and heels, she is infinitely respectable by local standards but still looks the epitome of everyone's expectation of 'Lady Di'.

One of the prettiest pictures ever taken of the radiant Princess Diana, here on a royal tour of Thailand, in 1988, having stolen the limelight by slipping a fresh local orchid bloom behind her ear. Eveningwear on an official tour really gave the Princess an opportunity to shine, and she relished the fairy-tale opportunity to dress up to the nines, embellished by millions of pounds worth of jewels. Her choice of French-born designer, Catherine Walker, was becoming ever more frequent, a close and fruitful friendship that produced most of Diana's key fashion moments.

The Order of the Garter service at Windsor Castle, in 1990, was one of many such occasions when Diana was on parade in her finest formal wear, complete with dramatic wide-brimmed hat, large black bag and matching gloves. This single-breasted, fuchsia-pink suit was made of the finest wool, tailored beautifully to flatter the figure and finished off with large, rope-edged buttons in the same shade of pink. The slanted flap pockets are carefully positioned to slim down the silhouette, and are the mark of an excellent tailor.

The Princess loved the fashion world, and it was a mutual affection. This picture shows her arriving at the Royal Albert Hall for the British Fashion Awards. Diana knew that whilst she may be a style leader elsewhere in the world, a specific fashion event like this, in a venue of such stature, required a sensational outfit, and as usual, Catherine Walker was her choice to create the gown. The ensemble was instantly known as 'the Elvis' because of the dramatic white colour and huge stand-up collar on the cropped, short-sleeved jacket, worn over a white, figure-hugging, strapless sheath dress. Both the dress and jacket were covered entirely in pearls, with an inch-wide border around the edges. It was instantly proclaimed a winner by the media, an outfit that would later take centre stage at the Christie's auction of dresses to raise money for her charities.

Above: A family wedding is always an occasion to dress up, but Princess Diana's audience went beyond the relatives in St George's Chapel, Windsor, to international magazines and newspapers. This was the marriage of Lady Helen Taylor, another very glamorous royal, the daughter of the Duke and Duchess of Kent. Princess Diana arrived in a striking skirt-suit, holding hands with nine-year-old son Harry who was also neatly turned out in blazer and grey flannels. Her single-breasted jacket was two-tone with a wide navy band at the waist, but mostly made up in bright green, and fastened with large gilt buttons.

Top left: Diana stepped out in the warm Sydney night, in 1996, wearing this asymmetrical, azure, full-length gown, looking like a goddess, in keeping with the statuesque styling of the one-shouldered dress. The cut, the colour and the silk satin made this creation a winner on every account.

Bottom left: Princess Diana had initiated the idea of selling off her most famous dresses to raise money for charity, and she wore this beautiful blue-beaded Catherine Walker dress to Christie's to publicise the auction. It was one of her last public appearances in the fashion arena, and she looked radiant at the success of the auction and funds raised for good causes. The dress itself was a sexy, low-cut style she had come to favour – especially following the triumph of the little black dress she wore to the Serpentine Gallery on the night Charles's admission of adultery was broadcast on television (above right). No longer restricted by royal protocol as to what she should wear and how she should behave, Diana was enjoying showing off her womanly figure.

'Recently we'd been seeing her in these incredibly slinky, sexy but not overly revealing evening dresses... She had a fantastic figure and great arms and she was happy to show them off.' Anna Wintour, *Vogue*.

Epilogue: Did she make a difference?

Of course Diana made a difference. If you doubt it, try going back to the beginning of this book and let the faces in the photographs give you their answer.

Of course she made mistakes too, though most of them can be excused or at least understood. Much of the time she was fighting for her existence as a royal figure, and she had to find her allies where she could. The miracle was that she didn't make more mistakes, find even worse allies or that she didn't go completely crazy under the strain.

One reason she didn't was that she never forgot that she *was* royal. As a Spencer she had her own noble lineage and historical roots as deep as anything the Windsors could claim and from this she drew great strength.

Diana's brand of royalty derived from being a princess – with or without the HRH prefix that she lost in 1996. She had become a princess through personal choice and, even if that choice wasn't to be the key to personal happiness, it was a decision that absolutely framed her view of the world. She carried it in her mind as surely as if it were in her DNA. And there was always the simple genetic fact that her son would one day be king.

There was another element in her royal credentials that marked her out from the celebrities with whom she was often identified. It was her determination to do her duty as a mainstream royal performer. This aspect is often overlooked. Remember at her wedding she chose the hymn 'I vow to thee my country', as traditional an anthem as the royal old guard could wish for. She was to have been our queen and often yearned, not to be a rebel, but for guidance and encouragement.

Her tragedy is that the words couldn't be found to keep her safely in the royal fold, or if they were she didn't hear them. The Royal Family's tragedy is that, as a result, the royal fold was an infinitely poorer place without her.

Her royal quality also derived from a physical and moral stature that would have cast her as a leader in any society, not from any particular personal virtue but from her ability to make life better for those at the bottom of the heap. She combined this feminine strength with an unerring eye for a tactical advantage, and a bravery that bordered on defiance.

All this marked her out, not to be a celebrity with a spasmodic appetite for fashionable causes, but to be a queen. And not just a benign symbol of constitutional evolution. Remember the reaction of the mourners at her funeral. To the crowds who watched her coffin pass, Diana was heir to something much more ancient and visceral.

A Boadicea – fallible but heroic. And probably, immortal…

For Gloria, Stephanie and Tracy,

Amelia and Phoebe

...and also for Bludgers everywhere

Special thanks to

Elspeth Henderson, Eddie Bell, Pat Lomax and Natalie Jerome